THE SEVEN BIG MYTHS
ABOUT THE
CATHOLIC CHURCH

CHRISTOPHER KACZOR

THE SEVEN BIG
MYTHS ABOUT THE
CATHOLIC CHURCH

Distinguishing Fact from Fiction about Catholicism

IGNATIUS PRESS   SAN FRANCISCO

Cover art:
The Whore of Babylon   — why this feminine symbol?
Colored woodcut from the Luther Bible, c. 1530
Bible Society, London, UK/The Bridgeman Art Library

Cover design by John Herreid

© 2012 by Ignatius Press, San Francisco
All rights reserved
ISBN 978-1-58617-791-1
Library of Congress Control Number 2012936914
Printed in the United States of America ∞

CONTENTS

INTRODUCTION

There are not more than 100 people in the world who truly hate the Catholic Church, but there are millions who hate what they perceive to be the Catholic Church.

—Bishop Fulton J. Sheen

An atheistic journalist, Peter Seewald, once asked Joseph Ratzinger, the future Pope Benedict XVI, the following question, how many paths are there to God? Cardinal Ratzinger replied, as many as there are people.[1] Each one of us has our own journey of life; each one of us has our own questions, challenges, and opportunities; each one of us is called by God to love him and to love other people so as to find happiness.

In the Christian perspective, God does not leave us alone or abandon us to wandering without aid in our search for happiness and meaning. Rather, God gives us a trustworthy way to return to him. God reveals to us the fullness of truth about our shared human condition in this journey and furnishes us with an illuminating Light

[1] Joseph Ratzinger, *Salt of the Earth: Christianity and the Catholic Church at the End of the Millennium; An Interview with Peter Seewald* (San Francisco: Ignatius Press, 1997), p. 8.

to guide us and give us strength on our path. Jesus is God's revelation to us both about who God is and about what it is to be fully human.

Jesus remains—two thousand years after his birth—a figure renowned for his wisdom, compassion, and courage. For Christians, Jesus is even more than a saintly sage. Christians accept as true Jesus' own description of himself, "I am the way and the truth and the life; no one comes to the Father but by me" (Jn 14:6).

Many people today call themselves Christians, yet believe that they can do without the Church. They love and admire Jesus, but they dislike and are suspicious of the Church. Archbishop Timothy Dolan of New York has talked about this phenomenon, making reference to the famous story of Saul, later Saint Paul, being knocked from his horse on the way to Damascus:

> Saul felt around and heard a voice, "Saul, Saul, why are you persecuting me?" "Who are you, Lord?" Saul asked. And the voice replied, "I am Jesus and you are persecuting me." Now my dear friends in Christ, parse those words carefully. Jesus did not say, "You are persecuting my disciples." He didn't say, "You're persecuting my followers." Jesus didn't say, "You're persecuting my friends." Or, "You're persecuting my church." No. "Why are you persecuting *me*?"... Jesus and his Church are one. Jesus equals his Church. Jesus and his Church are a package deal.... I'm afraid, we are now living in an era where people believe they can have Christ without his Church. People want a king without a kingdom. They want a shepherd with no flock. They want a spiritual family, sure, with God as their Father and Jesus as their brother and them as the only child. They want to believe without belonging. They

want a general without an army. They want spirituality
without religion. They want faith without the faithful. They
want Christ without his Church.[2]

Many people call themselves Christian but do not see
the importance of the Church. Indeed, they reject the
Church for a variety of reasons. Yet, Jesus sees a deep
unity between himself and his body, the Church. To accept
Jesus is to become a *part* of this body, a member of the
Church.

The biggest obstacle to people seeing this unity between
Christ and his Church is the sinfulness of the members
of the Church. As G. K. Chesterton said, "The only good
argument against Christianity is Christians." [3] The sins
of every member of the Church make the message of
Jesus less credible and injure the mission given by Jesus
to the Church to make disciples of all nations. These
sins, including the very grave sins of priests who sexually
abused minors and bishops who did not act properly to
prevent further abuse, impede the proclamation of the
message of Jesus. In these corrupt actions, the members
of the Church have separated themselves from Jesus, as
the apostles did when all but one abandoned Jesus during his Passion. These sins betray Jesus, as Peter once did
in denying Jesus three times. The denials of Jesus by his
followers have continued through the centuries. Sadly,
every Catholic can say with truth, "I have sinned through

[2] Archbishop Timothy Dolan, Los Angeles Prayer Breakfast, September
21, 2010.
[3] As cited by Peter Kreeft and Ronald Tacelli, *Handbook of Catholic Apol-
ogetics: Reasoned Answers to Questions of Faith* (San Francisco: Ignatius Press,
2009), p. 180.

my own fault, in my thoughts and in my words, in what I have done and what I have failed to do."

These sins do not, however, change the reality of the Church's unity with Jesus. The Church remains united with Jesus, that is, holy, because of the work and action of Christ in three dimensions. First, Jesus remains united with his Church in the seven sacraments—outward signs instituted by Christ and administered by the human ministers in the Church to give grace. These sacraments retain their power to transform the lives of the followers of Jesus whether the minister of the sacrament is a great saint or a great sinner. In a similar way, the words of Jesus as read in the Bible remain true, even if the person reading the words aloud is an evil person. The lack of worthiness of the minister cannot destroy the power of the biblical words or the power of the sacraments.

Secondly, the unity of Christ and the Church is evident in the saints, those who most fully receive his sacramental grace and actually live out his message. If the best argument against Christianity is (bad) Christians, then the best argument for Christianity is (good) Christians. Indeed, Christianity is properly measured not by its great sinners but by its great saints, for it is the saints who have lived out the Gospel message, not the great sinners. Would it be fair to judge a hospital by the patients who disregard doctor's orders and fail to take their medication? Would it be fair to judge a school by the students who do not pay attention in class and fail to do their homework? The Church's holiness, her unity with Jesus, is best seen in the saints, by those who most fully lived the message and sacramental life of the Church, by

Saint Francis of Assisi and by Mother Teresa, as well as by the holy people that we've known personally in our lives.

Finally, the unity of Christ and the Church is evident in the preservation of the Church from teaching as true what is false in terms of faith and morals. Christ came to reconcile us to the Father and to speak the truth to us in love. Unless there is an authentic interpreter of the message of Jesus, this message is in danger of being compromised. Jesus loved us enough to provide a living, authentic interpreter of the Gospel to ensure that his message would be transmitted faithfully in every age. Catholics believe this authentic interpretation is given by the teaching of the Church, especially the pope. The Holy Father, the Bishop of Rome, speaks with a living voice, responding to the signs of the times, and interpreting human experience, Scripture, Church councils, and his forefathers on the Petrine chair in light of present questions, needs, and concerns. Christ's Vicar on earth, despite personal weaknesses and limitations, safeguards the unity of the Church and, guided by the Spirit, has as a mission the continuing fathering of the Church here on earth. In this, every Vicar of Christ is like Peter before him who, although he denied the Lord three times, was still called to confirm his brethren and feed Christ's sheep.

It is important to recognize that the Church *never* claimed that her lay members or her priests and bishops would be free from wrongdoing. There is a difference between *infallibility* (inability to teach as true views that are false) and *impeccability* (inability to sin). The official and formal teaching of the Church, in certain limited situations, is infallible, but *no one* in the Church militant is impeccable. Popes, bishops, and priests can be as good or bad as anyone else. Infallibility also has nothing to do with Church governance. For example, serious mistakes have been made in terms of putting in the best possible person to be the next bishop of a diocese or expelling horrible priests from ministry.

Lord Macaulay once said: "After considerable study, and with some admitted regret as a Protestant, I must confess that I consider the Roman Catholic Church to be of divine origin because no mere human institution run with such knavish imbecility could have survived two weeks."[4] Scandal and sins by people inside the Church have been a sad reality for two thousand years and will continue until the end of time. But the guidance and power of the Holy Spirit is even more operative in the Church, from her very beginning until the end of time.

The proper responses to these wrongful acts was pointed out by Pope John Paul II, who apologized and repented for more than fifty different mistakes and bad actions done by the Church over the centuries. Individual Catholics too have an obligation to apologize, make amends, and seek to change their lives so as to follow the way of Jesus better.

Unfortunately, negative experiences with Catholics, especially those in positions of authority, have been an occasion for people to reject the Church. "Father McNellis,

[4] As quoted by Archbishop Timothy Dolan, Los Angeles Prayer Breakfast, September 21, 2010.

my parish priest, was so rude to me in confession, that I just left and never came back." "My third grade teacher, Sister Ignatius, was the meanest person that I have ever met, so I quit being Catholic." Anyone who has spent any length of time in a Catholic school, hospital, or parish can tell similar stories of greater or lesser failures by Catholic people—priests, sisters, and laity alike.

But, consider any other group of people. Recall your past interactions with physicians in the doctor's office or hospital. I've had many doctors who were uncaring, inattentive, and lacking in compassion, but it would be absurd for me to reason, "That's it. I'm not seeking medical attention ever again." Or consider students getting their education. I certainly had teachers who were unfair, unkind, and impatient. But it would have been ridiculous for me as a sophomore to conclude, "I've had enough of Mrs. Franklin. I'm dropping out of school." How many people have had negative interactions with people at the grocery store, but no one thereby declares that they no longer will buy food. Indeed, if we think about any group that we belong to with whom we have regular interactions, it would be impossible to go long in the group without conflicts, misunderstandings, and bad experiences with some fellow members. Despite these difficulties, it is good for us to belong, for we are not meant to live in utter isolation. If we still seek medical care despite bad doctors, if we still seek to learn despite bad teachers, if we still shop despite rude clerks, we should still belong to the Church despite the bad members of the Church. After all, if the Church were admit to her ranks only perfect and sinless members, we ourselves would not be allowed to join. The Church is a hospital for sinners, people just like us and even worse, with faults and foibles, who are called, with the help of God, to love God and neighbor better.

Although sinful behavior is probably the primary obstacle, the way to God through Christ and his Church is sometimes also blocked by various misunderstandings people have about what the Church believes and does. This book addresses some of those major misunderstandings. It is written to help dispel common myths that people believe about the Catholic Church, particularly about certain controversial questions that are significant today.

In the contemporary world, misinformation and myth abound in reference to certain key issues. Everyone "knows" the Church opposes happiness, freedom, and science. Everyone "knows" the Church hates women and homosexuals. Everyone "knows" contraception enhances love, and opposition to same-sex marriage is based on bigotry. And, of course, everyone "knows" of the pedophilia of most Catholics priests who, distorted by celibacy, sexually abuse children. No book can answer everyone's questions, objections, and concerns, but this work examines and clarifies seven of the most controversial and most common myths about the Catholic Church.

In writing this book, I think about people that I've known over the years, some of them dear, lifelong friends, whose names I've changed but who represent types of people that we probably all know. I think of Danny who became convinced that the Catholic Church undermines the true happiness and freedom of people and seems to be no less happy having gone. I think of my brilliant childhood friend, Angus. He is the youngest of a family of six and likes to argue with me about why the Church is wrong on birth control. Angus is also well versed in math and science. He thinks that there is a conflict between faith and reason, between science and Christianity. I think too about Colleen who views the Church as "against women". I think of my gay friend Mark who thinks the Church rejects him. These friends of mine, and so many others, have, sadly, serious misunderstandings that partially block their unity with Christ and his Church. These people deserve to know the truth about the important questions that they are asking. And in some cases, they would be aided by asking more questions rather than being satisfied with dogmatic acceptance of mythical perspectives of what the Church believes.

This book does not, of course, take on *all* the myths or misunderstandings; no single work could. In particular, this book does not address many misunderstandings that Protestant Christians have about Catholic Christians. Many of these misunderstandings are held by Evangelical Christians who share so much with Catholics in terms of basic beliefs—God's saving work through Jesus Christ, the importance of prayer and biblical study. However, certain Catholic beliefs and practices are viewed by Evangelicals as unbiblical or even antibiblical. Other books—in particular many works by Scott Hahn as well as Karl Keating's wonderful work *Catholicism and Fundamentalism*—address these important issues. Readers should look to these works for help in addressing the misunderstandings and myths that surround Evangelical-Catholic dialogue. However, many of these people can also benefit from a consideration of the issues treated in this book as well. I pray that whoever reads this work is able to take at least a few steps toward a closer relationship with God and his Church.

The First Big Myth

The Church Opposes Science:
The Myth of Catholic Irrationality

Many people believe that faith and reason, or religion and science, are locked in an irreconcilable war of attrition against one another. One must choose to be a person of learning, science, and reason, or choose to embrace religion, dogma, and faith alone. On this view, the Church opposes science, and if one embraces science, then one ought to reject the Church.

The scientific method looks to evidence to settle questions, so perhaps it would be fair to look at evidence to answer the question whether the Catholic Church is opposed to science and reason. If the Catholic Church were opposed to science, we would expect to find no or very few Catholic scientists, no sponsorship of scientific research by Catholic institutions, and an explicit distrust of reason in general and scientific reasoning in particular taught in official Catholic teaching. In fact, we find none of these things.

Historically, Catholics are numbered among the most important scientists of all time, including René Descartes, who discovered analytic geometry and the laws of refraction; Blaise Pascal, inventor of the adding machine, hydraulic press, and the mathematical theory of probabilities; Augustinian priest Gregor Mendel, who founded modern genetics; Louis Pasteur, founder of microbiology and creator of the first vaccine for rabies and anthrax; and cleric Nicolaus Copernicus, who first developed scientifically the view that the earth rotated around the sun. Jesuit priests in particular have a long history of scientific achievement; they

> contributed to the development of pendulum clocks, pantographs, barometers, reflecting telescopes and microscopes, to scientific fields as various as magnetism, optics and electricity. They observed, in some cases before anyone else, the colored bands on Jupiter's surface, the Andromeda nebula and Saturn's rings. They theorized about the circulation of the blood (independently of Harvey), the theoretical possibility of flight, the way the moon affected the tides, and the wave-like nature of light. Star maps of the southern hemisphere, symbolic logic, flood-control measures on the Po and Adige rivers, introducing plus and minus signs into Italian mathematics—all were typical Jesuit achievements, and scientists as influential as Fermat, Huygens, Leibniz and Newton were not alone in counting Jesuits among their most prized correspondents.[1]

The scientist credited with proposing in the 1930s what came to be known as the "Big Bang theory" of the origin of the universe was Georges Lemaître, a Belgian physicist and Roman Catholic priest. Alexander Fleming, the inventor of penicillin, shared his faith. More

---

[1] Jonathan Wright, *The Jesuits: Missions, Myths, and Histories* (London: HarperCollins, 2004), p. 189; quoted in Thomas Woods, *How the Catholic Church Built Western Civilization* (Washington, D.C.: Regnery Publishing, 2005), p. 100.

recently, Catholics constitute a good number of Nobel Laureates in Physics, Medicine, and Physiology, including Erwin Schrödinger, John Eccles, and Alexis Carrel. How can the achievements of so many Catholics in science be reconciled with the idea that the Catholic Church opposes scientific knowledge and progress?

One might try to explain such distinguished Catholic scientists as rare individuals who dared to rebel against the institutional Church, which opposes science. However, the Catholic Church as an institution funds, sponsors, and supports scientific research in the Pontifical Academy of Science and in the departments of science found in every Catholic university across the world, including those governed by Roman Catholic bishops, such as The Catholic University of America. This financial and institutional support of science by the Church began at the very birth of science in seventeenth-century Europe and continues today. Even Church buildings themselves were not only used for religious purposes but designed in part to foster scientific knowledge. As Thomas Woods notes:

> Cathedrals in Bologna, Florence, Paris, and Rome were designed in the seventeenth and eighteenth centuries to function as world-class solar observatories. Nowhere in the world were there more precise instruments for the study of the sun. Each such cathedral contained holes through which sunlight could enter and time lines (or meridian lines) on the floor. It was by observing the path traced out by the sunlight on these lines that researchers could obtain accurate measurements of time and predict equinoxes.[2]

---

[2] Woods, *Catholic Church Built Western Civilization*, p. 112.

In the words of J. L. Heilbron of the University of California, Berkeley, the "Roman Catholic Church gave more financial aid and social support to the study of astronomy over six centuries, from the recovery of ancient learning during the late Middle Ages into the Enlightenment, than any other, and probably, all other institutions." [3] This financial and social support extended also to other branches of scientific inquiry.

Such support is not only consistent with official Catholic teaching but is enthusiastically endorsed. On the Church's view, science and faith are complementary to each other and mutually beneficial. In 1988, Pope John Paul II addressed a letter to the Director of the Vatican Astronomical Observatory, noting, "Science can purify religion from error and superstition; religion can purify science from idolatry and false absolutes. Each can draw the other into a wider world, a world in which both can flourish." [4] As Nobel Laureate Joseph Murray notes, "Is the Church inimical to science? Growing up as a Catholic and a scientist—I don't see it. One truth is revealed truth, the other is scientific truth. If you really believe that creation is good, there can be no harm in studying science. The more we learn about creation—the way it emerged—it just adds to the glory of God. Personally, I've never seen a

---

[3] J. L. Heilbron, Annual Invitation Lecture to the Scientific Instrument Society, Royal Institution, London, December 6, 1995; quoted in ibid., p. 113.

[4] Letter of His Holiness John Paul II to the Reverend George V. Coyne, S.J., Director of the Vatican Observatory, June 1, 1988, http://www.vatican.va/holy_father/john_paul_ii/letters/1988/documents/hf_jp-ii_let_19880601_padre-coyne_en.html.

conflict."[5] In order to understand the complementarity of faith and science, indeed faith and reason more broadly, it is important to consider their relationship in greater depth.

A sign hung in Albert Einstein's office at Princeton University that read: "Not everything that can be counted counts; not everything that counts can be counted." Faith cannot be quantified and counted, like forces in physics or elements in chemistry, but that does not mean that faith is insignificant. Faith helps us to answer some of the most important questions facing mankind. As important as scientific discoveries can be, such discoveries do not touch on all of the inevitable questions facing us: What should I do? Whom should I love? What can I hope for? To answer questions such as these, science alone is not enough because science alone cannot answer questions that fall outside its empirical method. Rather, we need faith and reason operating together to answer such questions and to build a truly human community.

One reason that people view faith and science as in opposition is that they often view faith and reason more generally as in opposition. Our culture often pits faith against reason, as if the more faith-filled you are, the less reasonable you are. Faith and reason in the minds of so many people are polar opposites, never to be combined, and never to be reconciled. In this way, our culture often offers us false alternatives: live either by faith or by reason. To be religious is to reject reason; to be reasonable

[5] As quoted by Gabriel Meyer, "Pontifical Science Academy Banks on Stellar Cast", *National Catholic Register*, December 1–7, 1996, as cited on http://atheismexposed.tripod.com/nobelistsgod.htm.

is to reject religion. But like other false alternatives, e.g., "Did you stop beating your wife this week, or last week?" such thinking artificially limits our freedom. Rather than choosing between faith and reason, the Church invites us to harmonize our faith and our reason because both are vitally important to human well-being.

Developing a long tradition of Catholic reflection on the compatibility of faith and reason, Pope Benedict XVI seeks to unite what has so often become divided, by championing the full breadth of reason (including but not limited to scientific reasoning) combined with an adult faith. Rather than pitting faith against reason, the pope is calling for a reasonable faith and a faithful reason. From a Catholic perspective, the truths of faith and the truths of reason (including science) cannot in principle ever be opposed, because God is the ultimate Author of the book of Grace (revelation) as well as the book of Nature (philosophy and science). One ought not, therefore, choose between faith on the one hand and reason on the other, but rather one should seek to bring both faith and reason into a more fruitful collaboration.

In a Catholic view, since faith and reason are compatible, science—one particular kind of reasoning—and the Catholic religion are also compatible. Nevertheless, it is a commonly held view that one must choose between science and faith. Why is this? There are several core issues that drive this misunderstanding. First, Genesis claims that God created the world in seven days, but science indicates that the universe, including the earth, developed over billions of years. Secondly, Genesis talks about the first man, Adam, and the first woman, Eve, being created by God, as well as all the animals being created by God. Science indicates that all life—including human life—evolved over millions of years. Third, Bible stories are rife with miracles, but science has shown that miracles are impossible. Fourth, and most famously, the Catholic Church condemned Galileo. Finally, the Church's opposition to stem cell research is seen as anti-science. Each of these objections is commonly used to justify the claim that the Church opposes science.

First, let's consider the claim that in Genesis God created the world in seven days but science indicates that the universe, including the earth, developed over billions of years. In the Catholic tradition, the creation accounts in Genesis have been interpreted in a wide variety of ways. Both literal and figurative readings of Genesis are theologically acceptable for Catholics. Some theologians, such as Saint Ambrose, understood the Genesis account of creation in a literal way. But for the most part, Catholic theologians, including Saint Augustine, Saint Thomas Aquinas, Blessed John Henry Newman, Pope John Paul II, and Pope Benedict XVI, have interpreted Genesis as teaching the truth about creation in a nonliteral, nonscientific way.[6] Pope John Paul II puts the point as follows:

> The Bible itself speaks to us of the origin of the universe and its make-up, not in order to provide us with a scientific treatise, but in order to state the correct relationships

[6] On Pope Benedict's view on this topic (at least the views he expressed prior to his election as pope), see Joseph Cardinal Ratzinger, *In the Beginning . . . : A Catholic Understanding of the Story of Creation and the Fall*, trans. Boniface Ramsey (Grand Rapids, Mich.: Wm. B. Eerdmans, 1995).

of man with God and with the universe. Sacred Scripture wishes simply to declare that the world was created by God, and in order to teach this truth it expresses itself in the terms of the cosmology in use at the time of the writer.[7]

Dr. Scott Hahn has pointed out that we might misunderstand the point of the seven days spoken about in Genesis, if we do not understand that the ancient Hebrew word for *seven* is the same word used for "making a covenant". So, when it is said that God created the world in seven days, the text is communicating to its original readers that God has created the world in a covenantal relationship with the Divine.[8] Indeed, it was this idea—that the world is an orderly creation from an intelligent God—that led to the beginnings of science. For if the world is not intelligible and orderly, there would be no point in trying to understand its laws of operation, the laws of nature which scientific investigation seeks to discover.

Secondly, the incompatibility of Genesis and the evolution of species causes some people to think that religious belief is incompatible with science. If the first man, Adam, and the first woman, Eve, were created by God, as well as all the animals, then all life—including human life—did not evolve over millions of years. If all life evolved over millions of years, then there could not be a first man, Adam, a first woman, Eve, or a creation of animals directly by God.

[7] Pope John Paul II, to the Pontifical Academy of Science, "Cosmology and Fundamental Physics", October 3, 1981, http://www.ewtn.com/library/PAPALDOC/JP2COSM.HTM.

[8] Scott Hahn, *A Father Who Keeps His Promises: God's Covenant Love in Scripture* (Ann Arbor, Mich.: Charis Books, 1998), pp. 140–44.

As noted, the Catholic Church does not generally require that individual Scripture verses be interpreted in one sense rather than another. Individual believers and theologians may come to different understandings of a particular passage but remain Catholics in good standing. So, one could believe with Saint Ambrose that Genesis provides a play-by-play account of exactly how God did things over seven 24-hour days. Or, one could believe with Saint Augustine, Saint Thomas Aquinas, Blessed John Henry Newman, Pope John Paul II, and Pope Benedict XVI that Genesis is not properly interpreted in this literalistic way. If one interprets Genesis in the ways suggested by the non-literal view, then there is no contradiction in believing both in Genesis and in evolution as a way for accounting for the physical development of man provided one believes in a first man and first woman, from whom mankind descended and inherited original sin (see *Humani Generis*, no. 27).[9] Of course, the Catholic Church does not require that Catholics believe in evolution or any other view taught by any given scientist. However, if one believes in evolution, then one can also—as did Pope John Paul II—remain a faithful Catholic.[10]

A third problem that gives rise to difficulties for some people is that miracles are found in the Bible, but science is incompatible with belief in miracles. By *miracle*, I mean a supernatural intervention by God into the normal course of events. Is belief in miracles incompatible with science? To answer this question, it is important to

[9] Pope John Paul II, "Truth Cannot Contradict Truth", Address of Pope John Paul II to the Pontifical Academy of Sciences (October 22, 1996).
[10] Ibid.

distinguish science or the scientific method from what is called philosophical naturalism. The scientific method looks for natural causes to explain things that have happened. Philosophical naturalism, a *philosophical* theory, not a *scientifically* justified view, holds that there are only natural causes and no supernatural (divine) causes. Scientists can conduct their scientific investigations with or without a belief in philosophical naturalism. If God the Creator exists, then naturalism is false because a Creator God is a supernatural cause. If there is a Creator with power over the entire universe, then miracles are possible, for God could intervene in his creation. Indeed, science could only prove that miracles cannot happen, *if* it proved that there is no God. But science has not and cannot prove such a claim, since the realm of science is limited to the empirically verifiable, and God—at least as understood by most believers—is not a material being but a spiritual being.

Fourth, and most famously, many people believe that the Catholic Church is antagonistic to science because of the condemnation of Galileo Galilei. This notorious and complicated conflict—the subject of many scholarly books—is partially based on scientific disputes but also has much to do with the conflicts of personality, politics, and theology of the time. Galileo's view that the earth rotated around the sun was not the central issue. Heliocentrism was held by many people of the time, including Jesuit priests in good standing. More central to the Galileo controversy was whether Galileo broke agreements he had made about in what manner to teach his views. Through his polemical writings, Galileo alienated one-time friends and gave rivals an opportunity to undermine him. His work *Dialogue Concerning the Two Chief World Systems* was widely understood to mock the pope, a one-time friend and sponsor. Galileo did not limit himself to scientific claims on the basis of a view at the time lacking conclusive proof, but also insisted on challenging the dominant interpretations of Scripture at the time, which held that the sun rotated around the earth.[11] Thus, both influential theologians as well as scientists turned against Galileo. If Galileo had presented his views with greater modesty about his claims, it is likely that there would have been no condemnation.

Nevertheless, it is true that ecclesial authorities wrongly condemned Galileo's heliocentricism, which was in 1633 not yet scientifically demonstrated. Galileo's view was condemned because of an overly literal interpretation of a certain passage in Scripture. This erroneous condemnation could have been avoided if the theologians involved had remembered the methods of biblical interpretation propounded by Saint Augustine and Saint Thomas Aquinas, who recognized that Scripture often speaks the truth about creation in a nonliteral, nonscientific way. Pope John Paul II wrote:

> Thanks to his intuition as a brilliant physicist and by relying on different arguments, Galileo, who practically invented the experimental method, understood why only the sun could function as the centre of the world, as it was then known, that is to say, as a planetary system. The error of the theologians of the time, when they maintained the centrality of

---

[11] As noted by Woods, *Catholic Church Built Western Civilization*, pp. 71–72.

the Earth, was to think that our understanding of the physical world's structure was, in some way, imposed by the literal sense of Sacred Scripture.[12]

Indeed, even today people still speak, as does Scripture, about "the sun rising", even though strictly speaking it is not the sun that rises but the earth that turns, causing it to appear that the sun rises.

In any case, Pope John Paul II acknowledged that the ecclesial judicial authorities in the trial of Galileo were wrong. These errors of a disciplinary and judicial nature were not a formal part of Catholic teaching. Then, as now, Church officials can and do make errors—unfortunately sometimes serious errors—in terms of discipline and order within the Church community. Church infallibility only applies to official teachings of faith and morals, not to assigning the best bishop to a particular place, nor to making wise decisions about political matters, nor to determining who can and ought to teach certain topics. The condemnation of Galileo was an erroneous decision in a matter of judicial order in the Christian community, but it does not have to do with official teaching of faith and morals.

One final controversy is the alleged opposition to science seen by Richard Dawkins. Dawkins writes, "He [Pope Benedict] is an enemy of science, obstructing vital stem cell research, on grounds not of morality but of

---

[12] Pope John Paul II, "Fidei Depositum", *L'Osservatore Romano*, no. 44 (1264), November 4, 1992, as cited by Daniel N. Robinson, Gladys M. Sweeney, Richard Gill, *Human Nature in Its Wholeness: A Roman Catholic Perspective* (Washington, D.C.: The Catholic University of America Press, 2006), p. 169.

pre-scientific superstition." [13] In other words, the Church opposes science because she opposes embryonic stem cell research that involves destroying human embryos. Stem cell research is viewed as a promising means of fighting disease and promoting human well-being, but the Church, in Dawkins' view, stands in the way of this progress.

It is important to begin responding to Dawkins' accusation with the common ground shared by all people of good will. Indeed, everyone agrees, including Dawkins, that we should not kill innocent people, even if killing them might benefit other people or bring about an advance in scientific knowledge. The Tuskegee experiment in which African-American males were research subjects without their consent and to their detriment is universally condemned. Similarly, the research done by Dr. Josef Mengele on various human patients, or rather victims, in Auschwitz cannot be justified regardless of the scientific progress that was an alleged goal of the experiments. It is a basic principle of ethics that persons should not be harmed without their consent in scientific research in order potentially to benefit other people.

It is this principle, together with modern science, that has led the Catholic Church to oppose embryo research that kills human embryos. If human embryos have basic human rights as do other human persons, then embryonic research that involves killing human embryos is wrong. It was actually science overcoming "pre-scientific superstition" that brought the Catholic Church to the defense of human life from conception. In ancient times, Aristotle taught that the human person arose only 40 to 90 days after the union of the man and the woman in sexual intercourse. Aristotle thought, and this view was a common one until the nineteenth century, that the menses of the woman was "worked on" by the fluid ejaculated by the man to form a human being, some 40 days after the sexual union in the case of a male and 90 days in the case of a female.

Contemporary biology has shown that this understanding of how human reproduction takes place is radically mistaken. Sperm and egg are the gametes of sexual reproduction, not the menses and the entire ejaculated fluid. There is not a different time period for the formation of male and female children, nor does the seminal fluid continue to work for weeks and weeks to inform the menses. Rather, egg and sperm unite so as to create a new, individual, living, whole human person which passes through various stages—zygotic, fetal, infant, toddler, adolescent, adult—of human development.

Is there any reason to think that the human embryo is alive? To live is to have self-generated activities. The activities of proportionate growth and increase of specialization of cells contributing to the good of the whole organism indicate that the embryo is a *living* being. Further, it is clear that the embryo can die, but only living things can die, so the embryo must be living.

Is the living embryo also *human*? Since the embryo arises from a human mother and a human father, what species could it be other than human? Coming as it does from a human mother and a human father, made of human

genetic tissues organized as a living being, and progress-
ing along the trajectory of human development, the newly
conceived human embryo is biologically and genetically
one of us. This new living, growing being is a member of
the species *homo sapiens*, a member of the human family.
This human being is genetically new, that is, distinct from
both mother and father. The embryo is not a part of the
mother (as is obvious when the embryo is in a petri dish
and not in utero), but rather is made from part of the
mother (her ovum) and part of the father (his sperm).
This new person is an individual whose genetic makeup
and very existence is not the same as the mother's or father's
or anyone else's. There is nothing "pre-scientific" about
the Church's view that the human embryo is a human
being; indeed, this view is confirmed by the findings of
science which overturned the long-accepted prescientific
views of Aristotle on reproduction.

Now, should very young human persons, including
human embryos, be protected by law and welcomed in
life? This is a moral question, not a scientific question.
Science attempts to discover what is the case; ethics attempts
to discover what should be the case in terms of human
choices. Should the human embryo be protected as are
human persons at later stages of development? I have
explored this question at great length in a book called
*The Ethics of Abortion: Women's Rights, Human Life, and the
Question of Justice*. Looking at every single pro-choice objection of which I was aware, I found that there is no rational justification for not according every human—including
those in the embryonic stage of development—equal basic
rights, including the right not to be intentionally killed

in the hopes of benefiting other people's health. By contrast, defenders of abortion and lethal embryonic stem cell research hold that it is permissible to kill some human beings in order to benefit others. However, *neither* view is "scientific". Science qua science cannot settle the question of which human beings should be accorded human rights and welcomed into the human community.

Dawkins is also mistaken that the Church obstructs vital stem cell research. The Church opposes research—stem cell or otherwise—that involves the intentional killing of human embryos. Stem cell research that does *not* involve killing embryos is not only permitted by the Church but even funded by the Church, which has held at least two international conferences on stem cell research and has also funded research on adult stem cells undertaken at the University of Maryland School of Medicine. This research, using stem cells from adults or umbilical cords, has actually been developed into treatments that have already saved human lives. To date, despite billions of dollars, embryonic stem cell research has not led to one cure or a single effective treatment. The Church does not oppose stem cell research as such, but only opposes any kind of research that involves killing humans.

At this point, we are in a position to come to a *prima facie* judgment about the question of whether the Church opposes science. On the one hand, we have the many Catholic scientists of distinction, from the beginning of the use of the scientific method until now, who argue that there is no conflict between their faith and their pursuit of science. We have the institutional Church sponsoring scientific endeavors of all kinds, at Catholic universities around the world, in the construction of cathedrals, and at the Vatican itself. We also have the explicit Catholic teaching that faith and reason are not opposed but rather complementary, and that scientific reasoning and faith are mutually enriching. On the other hand, we have the trial and condemnation of Galileo. The Galileo case appears, against the larger background of Catholic teaching and practice, as an unfortunate aberration from the norm. However, both Galileo himself—who remained a faithful Catholic all his life—and those involved in his trial, such as Saint Robert Bellarmine, agreed that there can never be a true conflict between science and faith. Apparent but not real conflicts can arise through a mistaken interpretation of faith (as was made by those who condemned Galileo), a misunderstanding of science (e.g., that science requires denying miracles), or both. It is therefore a myth—albeit a persistent myth—that the Church opposes science.

The Second Big Myth

The Church Opposes
Freedom and Happiness:
The Myth of Catholic Indifference
to Earthly Welfare

Many people suspect, and some actually say, that the Catholic Church opposes freedom and happiness. The Church says no to so many actions deemed by contemporary people as, if not essential, then at least conducive to our freedom to pursue happiness. This leads people to view the Church as a nefarious force, undermining human well-being. For example, Richard Dawkins writes, "What major institution most deserves the title of greatest force for evil in the world? In a field of stiff competition, the Roman Catholic Church is surely up there among the leaders." [1]

In trying to answer the question of whether the Church opposes freedom and happiness, it is essential to define what exactly is meant by both *freedom* and *happiness*. These words are often used ambiguously. Let's begin with happiness. We all want to be happy. Every day, in whatever

---

[1] Richard Dawkins, "Ratzinger Is an Enemy of Humanity", September 22, 2010, http://www.guardian.co.uk/commentisfree/belief/2010/sep/22/ratzinger-enemy-humanity (accessed December 8, 2010).

we do, we seek this goal—one that we share with every other person on the planet. But what exactly is happiness? And how can we find it?

To discover the answer to these questions, and so as not to bias our investigation from the start either for or against religious belief in general or Catholic belief in particular, let's turn to psychology and philosophy for some answers. Psychologists have been studying what makes people happy for decades. Indeed, there is an entire branch of psychology, called "positive psychology", devoted to precisely the study of human flourishing and happiness. Psychologists study this topic in various ways. One way is to have people wear beepers, and then, at the prompting of the researchers during the course of the day, the research subjects write down the degree to which they are happy. Psychologists study rates of depression and cases of suicide and attempted suicide. They observe people and draw conclusions from their smiles and laughter or frowns and tears about whether or not they are happy. Over several decades, in thousands of studies across the world, researchers have gathered much evidence about what does and does not bring human happiness. Sonja Lyubomirsky, in her book *The How of Happiness: A Scientific Approach to Getting the Life You Want*, examines hundreds of these empirical studies. She concludes that about 50 percent of individual differences in happiness are determined by genes, about 10 percent by life circumstances, and 40 percent by our chosen intentional activities.[2]

---

[2] Sonja Lyubomirsky, *The How of Happiness: A Scientific Approach to Getting the Life You Want* (London: Penguin, 2007), p. 20.

Some people, it turns out, are naturally more optimistic, joyful, and upbeat. Therefore, we should not feel bad if we find ourselves with a less cheerful temperament than others. At the same time, circumstances of life—great wealth, good weather, and a promotion at work—have a relatively minor effect on our long-term level of happiness. The scientific evidence indicates that changing our circumstances will only slightly affect our outlook, as we quickly adapt to our new circumstances. Yet, while we cannot alter our genetic background, and altering our circumstances will not make much of a lasting difference to our happiness, we can dramatically change our intentional activities—that is, our goals in life. Engaging in work toward meaningful goals that strengthen our relationships with others can make us much happier. And regardless of our circumstances, we can become happier if we choose our priorities wisely. It turns out that our intentional activities can help us find or can inhibit finding happiness.

Drawing on the work of philosophers and psychologists, Robert J. Spitzer's book *Healing the Culture* distinguishes four different kinds of intentional activities—four different kinds of goals or levels of happiness.[3] Level-one happiness is bodily pleasure obtained by drink, food, drugs, or sex, etc. Level-two happiness pertains to competitive advantage in terms of money, fame, power, popularity, or other material goods. Level-three happiness involves loving and serving other people, and therefore avoiding

[3] Robert Spitzer, S.J., *Healing the Culture* (San Francisco: Ignatius Press, 2000).

harming others. And level-four happiness is found in loving and serving God. Although we desire happiness of each kind, not every level provides equal and lasting contentment.

In life, we are often faced with a choice between one level of happiness or another. For example, the Olympic athlete chooses success in athletics over pleasures of the body, which might be found in abusing drugs or alcohol. We can have more level-one happiness if we sleep late on Monday morning, but we would sacrifice level-two happiness because we wouldn't be able to earn money at work. (Some people combine both kinds of devotion—to bodily pleasure *and* money, power, and fame—into an alluring and attractive mix: the life of the celebrity.) Some people are willing to give up exclusive devotion to bodily pleasure in the pursuit of happiness through power, prestige, fame, and money. They will give up drugs, booze abuse, and carousing in order to win the competition for more money, more power, and more fame. Often, but not always, we must choose between love of bodily pleasure and love of winning more money, shopping, power, or fame. Or, we could gain more of a certain kind of happiness by cheating others out of their money; however, then we would be sacrificing a higher level of happiness because being unfair to others is the opposite of helping them. Since we often have to prioritize one activity over another, it makes sense to think through what kind of activities will truly lead to lasting happiness.

The level-one way to happiness is by means of good food, drugs, alcohol, and sex. Those pursuing these envision the "good life" as living like Hugh Hefner or his female equivalent. In this view, bodily pleasure is the source of our ultimate fulfillment. Happiness consists in drink, dope, sex, and whatever else makes our bodies feel good.

The first level of happiness—pleasures of the senses—has several advantages. It is easy to get; it arrives fairly quickly; and it can be intense. Level-one happiness, though, leaves almost as quickly as it arrives. In addition, we build a tolerance to certain things that bring us this level of happiness, so that more is needed to achieve the same degree of enjoyment. For example, as our bodies grow accustomed to drinking alcohol, we develop a tolerance to it so that greater and greater amounts are needed to achieve the intoxication formerly achieved through a smaller amount of alcohol. Unfortunately, many of these pleasures can lead to addictions, and the addict's enslavement is the opposite of real happiness. Finally, this lowest level of happiness is somewhat superficial. Our search for meaning, significance, and making a real difference to the world is not satisfied at level one. We all enjoy bodily happiness, but we also want to achieve something more meaningful and important in life than merely feeling good.

Philosophers Germain Grisez and Robert Nozick have proposed a thought experiment that suggests we all want more than just bodily pleasure. Imagine scientists construct a pleasure box in which you could enter and have your brain electronically stimulated so as to experience ever-increasing levels of pleasure. Feeding tubes would keep you indefinitely alive so that you could live the rest of your life in this box with nonstop pleasure and no bodily pain. Would you want to enter into this box permanently? If you do choose to enter the pleasure box, you would have no real friends, you would not be there to help your family when they needed you, and you would also never learn anything again or experience anything in the real world. Perfect pleasure at the expense of everything else you want. Who would want to be locked away permanently in the pleasure box? This thought experiment indicates that we all want much more than even perfect level-one happiness.

Level-two happiness gives greater meaning and significance than level-one. Level-two happiness is winning in any given competition for a social good. It involves not just keeping up with the Joneses, but also surpassing them—in money, fame, popularity, or status. We celebrate such achievements as a culture—the valedictorian, the star athlete, the millionaire. But will such success lead to lasting happiness?

Let's take money as an example of a level-two goal. It turns out that more money *can* make you much happier—if you live in abject poverty. If you have no clothes to keep you warm, no food for your children, and no roof over your head at night, money for these basic provisions greatly improves reported happiness. For people who don't eat three meals a day and whose housing has been swept away by a hurricane, additional money can make a great difference in happiness.

Once people are no longer desperate to meet their basic needs, however, the role of money shifts significantly. In his book *The Pursuit of Happiness*, psychologist David Myers points to evidence that once a person escapes from dire poverty, additional amounts of money do not significantly increase happiness. In other words, once a person has the basic necessities, more money does not lead to more happiness. Myers maintains that

> whether we base our conclusion on self-reported happiness, rates of depression, or teen problems, *our becoming much better off over the last thirty years has not been accompanied by one iota of increased happiness and life satisfaction.* It's shocking because it contradicts our society's materialistic assumptions, but how can we ignore the hard truth: *Once beyond poverty, further economic growth does not appreciably improve human morale.* Making more money—that aim of so many graduates and other American dreamers . . . does not breed bliss.[4]

Although most Americans have the basic needs of life met (our society battles obesity rather than starvation), we all want more in material goods. Advertisers spend billions of dollars a year feeding our appetites for things to buy. Most of these items we do not really, properly speaking, "need" and would never have wanted at all were it not for the daily barrage of various kinds of ads.

If you compare a person making $30,000 a year, another making $100,000, and a third making $500,000, there is likely little difference in self-reported happiness or levels of depression. Most people, when asked, will say that they need just a little bit more money to be comfortable, around 10 percent more. Whether people make $30,000 per year, $60,000 per year, $120,000 per year, or more than $1,000,000 per year, they tend to think that that 10 percent more will make a difference. When they do get that 10 percent, which typically happens over the

---

[4] David G. Myers, *The Pursuit of Happiness: Who Is Happy—and Why* (New York: William Morrow and Co., 1992), p. 44.

course of a few years worth of raises, they want just another 10 percent, and so on, *ad infinitum.*

Why don't additional amounts of money make us happier in a lasting way? Empirical research indicates that we eventually get used to whatever level of financial success we achieve and then begin to seek higher levels of affluence.[5] We tend to compare ourselves with those who are richer than we are, rather than the vast numbers who live in poverty. The average middle-class person in the United States or Europe today enjoys luxury and comfort unknown even to medieval kings. Indeed, at all levels of wealth, from the modestly to the tremendously wealthy, people tend to compare themselves to those who are just ahead of them in riches. Parents making $40,000 a year tend not to say, "Wow, we are doing so much better than 95 percent of the entire world. We have one TV and one car. We have a computer. We're doing amazingly well financially." Rather, they tend to look at those with two cars and three TVs, who in turn compare themselves to those with newer cars, bigger houses, and the latest plasma-screen TVs, and so on.

But maybe having, not just more money, but *lots* more money would lead to true happiness. Perhaps, if we had not just 10 to 15 percent more but millions more, then we'd be happy. Again, empirical research does not support this view. Lottery winners—after the shock wears off—report being no happier than they were before winning. Indeed, some seem less happy. In his book *Myths, Lies and*

---

[5] John Stossel, *Myths, Lies and Downright Stupidity* (New York: Hyperion, 2006), p. 269.

Downright Stupidity, John Stossel interviews Curtis Sharpe, lottery winner of five million dollars, and Sherry Gagliardi, winner of twenty-six million dollars:

> *Curtis Sharpe*: For a time, it seemed like I was in a dream world, you know?
> *Stossel*: Did you come down to earth?
> *Curtis Sharpe*: Oh, yes. I came down, you know. I came down to earth. I got divorced from my first wife and married my second wife, and I spent a lot of money on the wedding, you know.
> *Stossel*: A hundred thousand dollars on a grand wedding.
> *Curtis Sharpe*: Yes, that didn't last five years. You know what I'm saying?
> *Sherry Gagliardi*: I was numb for three years.
> *Stossel*: But you must have been happy.
> *Sherry Gagliardi*: Yes and no. I got a divorce two years after we had won. People have a misconception about having money. You go out and you go, "Oh, that's what I want, I'll buy it." Well, a couple weeks later, it's like, you know, that emptiness comes back. Then what?
> *Curtis Sharpe*: I mean, how many suits can I wear? How many hats can I wear? You know what I am saying?[6]

Perhaps the lottery winners were not happy because they didn't earn their money, and so they don't really appreciate it. Maybe if you earn millions and millions of dollars, this leads to deep happiness. However, studies of Fortune 500 executives found they had only average levels of happiness, and 37 percent of these ultra-wealthy business leaders are less happy than the average person. Vast sums of money, whether earned or won, simply cannot make us happy. If you compare a lottery winner and a paraplegic a year after

[6] Ibid., pp. 268–69.

the fateful events occurred, you would know virtually nothing about their levels of happiness. If you compare the CEO of a Fortune 500 company and the janitor who cleans his office, given this knowledge alone, you would have no way to know which person is happier.

What is true of money is also true of other goals sought at level two, including fame, power, prestige, popularity, and possessions. Whatever level of success we achieve in terms of these things, we quickly adapt to and seek still more. We tend to compare ourselves to those who have more fame, power, prestige, popularity, or possessions than we do, rather than those who have less. Finally, our desires cannot be perfectly satisfied by fame, power, prestige, popularity, or possessions. And we will only find true happiness elsewhere.

These findings by contemporary psychologists are quite a relief. Our culture tends to equate the "good life", a happy life, with the "Lifestyles of the Rich and Famous", a lifestyle well beyond the reach of most people. Few of us will be as wealthy, powerful, famous, and popular as celebrities. But happiness is not therefore out of reach.

What then does contemporary positive psychology say about what happiness is? Once a person has escaped dire poverty, four things matter in particular: (1) meaningful activity, (2) good relationships with others, (3) personal control, and (4) religious ties.[7] Making a similar point, Aristotle taught that happiness is activity in accordance with virtue in a complete life enjoyed with friends. In order for

[7] Ibid., pp. 267–74.

us to be objectively happy, we need to engage in activities that accord with virtue, such as justice toward others.

We can talk about these things in terms of the deeper levels of happiness, levels three and four. Without choosing higher levels of happiness, even if we subjectively feel good (for a while), we are missing out on objectively being happy. Level-three happiness does not consist in simply feeling good (level one) or even "having it all" (level two), but rather in making a contribution to the well-being of others. Just as we all have level-one and level-two desires, so too we all want to make a difference in the world. We want truly to love other people and be loved by them. We want to make their lives better, to be of service, to show our care and love for others. At level three, the concern is not to be "better" than others in terms of wealth, power, or prestige, but rather to make a lasting and meaningful contribution to their well-being. The goal of level-three happiness is to help people, so those seeking to live at level three avoid the opposite activity, namely, harming people. At level three, we choose meaningful activity in order to foster the well-being of others and enhance our relationships with them.

Finally, at level four, our happiness is found in loving God and being loved by God. Again, we choose meaningful activity in order to enhance our relationship with God and with other people. Level three and level four really go together insofar as no one can claim really to love God if he does not also love the image of God, the human person. So, does it follow that if a person is an atheist, then the person must not be truly happy? Certainly, some atheists believe that they have found true happiness.

An atheist certainly can have happiness at levels one, two, and three. But if someone does not believe that God exists, then it does not seem possible for that person to have a loving relationship with God, so that person cannot have level-four happiness. Similarly, if someone did not believe that other people existed, that person would deprive himself of level-three happiness.

With the conception of happiness depicted by positive psychology in mind, we are now in a better position to answer the question: Does the Catholic Church oppose or support happiness? Let's begin with helping people find happiness by escaping from dire poverty. Worldwide, and also in the United States, few institutions provide more help to the poor and the needy than does the Catholic Church. For example, in the United States,

> the Catholic Charities network is the nation's fourth largest non-profit, according to *The NonProfit Times*. The combined revenue of the Catholic Charities network from all sources, public and private, was $2.69 billion in 2000. Nearly 90 percent of these funds were spent on programs and services, making the Catholic Charities network one of the country's most efficient charities. Today, the Catholic Charities network—more than 1,600 local agencies and institutions nationwide—provide help, sometimes with government funding, and create hope for 6,597,998 in 2003, regardless of religious, social, or economic backgrounds, thanks to the dedication of more than 51,000 staff and 175,000 volunteers.[8]

[8] United States Conference of Catholic Bishops, "The Catholic Church in America—Meeting Real Needs in Your Neighborhood", http://www.old.usccb.org/comm/2006CIPFinal.pdf (accessed July 25, 2011).

In the United States, in 2003 alone, Catholic Charities provided food for 6,597,998 people; clothing, utilities, and utilities assistances for 1,521,597 people; emergency shelter for 201,653 people in need, such as victims of domestic abuse and runaways; and various "community building services" such as care for the elderly, job-readiness training, and disability services for 3,108,839 people.[9]

One of the most effective ways to help people to escape poverty is through education, and the Catholic Church sponsors grade schools, high schools, and universities throughout the world. In the United States alone, "The Catholic Church runs the largest network of private schools in the United States. Over 2.5 million students are enrolled in its 6,386 elementary schools and 1,203 high schools."[10] These schools, particularly the grade schools and high schools, have an excellent record of helping minority students to excel and escape a life of poverty.

Another significant way people's lives are enhanced, both in terms of escaping poverty and in terms of control, is by means of health care. Again, the Catholic Church sponsors medical research and hospitals worldwide: "615 Catholic hospitals account for 12.5% of community hospitals in the United States, and over 15.5% of all U.S. hospital admissions.... In addition to hospitals, the Catholic health care network also includes 404 health care centers and 1,509 specialized homes."[11] These services help millions of people worldwide each year be healthy enough to be able to work, and thus to arise from poverty.

[9] Ibid.
[10] Ibid.
[11] Ibid.

So, aside from helping people escape from poverty, how does the Catholic Church relate to the intentional activities or four levels of happiness described by Spitzer? Let's begin with bodily pleasure. Does the Church oppose level-one happiness? Not in the least. The pleasure that comes from good activities is a good thing. There would be something wrong if a husband and wife did not enjoy making love, or if a hungry person did not enjoy eating food. Drinking alcohol, enjoying food, and having sex can contribute to our well-being, and the pleasure involved stimulates us to seek them. In the words of Hilaire Belloc, "Wherever the Catholic sun doth shine, There's always laughter and good red wine. At least I've always found it so. Benedicamus Domino!" [12]

However, it is possible that the pursuit of bodily pleasure can be disordered. Put differently, in some circumstances, achieving level-one happiness can undermine the deeper levels of happiness. Abusing alcohol, food, or sex can undermine our own well-being and the well-being of others. The Church warns against such abuse in urging the faithful to avoid lust, gluttony, and drunkenness— for their own sakes as well as for the sake of others. Insofar as we seek bodily pleasure in such a way that is compatible with the love of God and love of neighbor, bodily pleasure is good. Insofar as we seek bodily pleasure in such a way that is incompatible with the love of God and love of neighbor, bodily pleasure undermines our true happiness.

[12] As cited by Michael Leach, *Why Stay Catholic? Unexpected Answers to Life-Changing Questions* (Chicago, Ill.: Loyola Press, 2011), p. 22.

Just as she does not oppose level-one happiness, so too the Church does not oppose level-two happiness. It is *good* to try to win in competitions, be they athletic, financial, or social, and winning in these competitions is also good. There is nothing wrong whatsoever with money, power, fame, or prestige, or with wanting them.

However, like the pursuit of pleasure, our love for level-two goods can become disordered so that it trumps love for God or love for neighbor. Perhaps, if we look in depth at one of the seven deadly sins condemned by the Church, it might become clearer how violation of God's law (sin) is simultaneously and necessarily also a violation of our own happiness. Let's consider greed. Greed is the disordered love of riches. We should love God above all things and our neighbor as ourselves, but we can begin to love money more than God and more than our neighbor. Greed (or avarice) is also one of the seven deadly sins. Like pride, lust, gluttony, sloth, anger, and envy, greed is sometimes called a "deadly" or "capital" sin because it gives rise to other sins.

I still remember my childhood picture Bible, which showed a shiny golden calf with people bowing down before it—a colorful depiction of the idolatry into which the ancient Israelites fell after Moses led them out of Egypt (Ex 32). The story struck me as incredibly strange for two reasons. First, I wondered why anyone would be so ridiculous as to worship a golden calf. Obviously, the gold statue was not really a living god. Second, I wondered why God would care so much about what they did. They weren't hurting anyone (were they?). It may be silly to worship a calf of gold, but why would God be concerned? Likewise, why should the Church condemn greed?

As an adult, I know from personal experience that the temptation to worship money rather than God is not limited to ancient Israel. People in our society are unlikely to bow down before a golden calf, but almost everyone in our society is tempted by greed in one of its forms. Today, greed often takes the form of consumerism and overwork. Consumerism is a view of the human person that reduces us to what we buy and consume. It is captured by the motto "He who dies with the most toys wins." The workaholic's greed, on the other hand, is not in consuming but in producing. "He who makes the most money wins." Both the shopaholic and the workaholic are, practically speaking, materialists. What really counts, the ultimate goal of life, is what can be bought and sold.

Of course, money and material goods are not evil but good. Indeed, we really do need money—or at least what Thomas Aquinas called "natural wealth" such as food, clothing, and shelter—to survive. We use what Thomas called "artificial wealth" such as cash, credit cards, or coins to purchase natural wealth. There is absolutely nothing wrong with wanting to secure the physical well-being of yourself and your loved ones through the use of money. In fact, that desire is good.

However, a healthy desire for natural wealth, and by extension artificial wealth, can grow into an unnatural and unhealthy desire for riches. But what exactly is wrong with desiring money too much? Put in the biblical context, what difference does it make *to God* if the ancient

Israelites worship a golden calf? Why should he care if people love money more than God and neighbor?

God cares about these matters because he cares about us. Exaggerated love of money does not hurt God—it does not diminish God himself in the least if we do not worship him. No, excessive love of money hurts *us*.

First, greed often leads to actions that are obviously harmful to our neighbor, such as stealing and cheating. When love of riches grows too strong, other sins typically follow: neglecting family to pursue career, donating little or nothing to charity, leaving inappropriately meager tips for help staff, cheating on tax returns, leaving no information after damaging a parked car, becoming unreasonably angry when money is lost or stolen, devoting unreasonable time and attention to financial matters, outright stealing, lying to get more money, taking financial advantage of people, falsifying insurance claims, and looking down on people who are poor. In other words, greed often thwarts our level-three happiness, in that it leads to the harm of others rather than the service of others. But even if avarice did not lead to additional sins against others, it would still be harmful to us. Simply put, if we love money more than we love God and other people, we make ourselves—usually sooner rather than later—miserable. Even if we had more money than Bill Gates, we still would not be happy without friendship with God and others.

God cares about greed because it undermines our true happiness. When we put making or spending money ahead of loving him, we lose out on an essential aspect of our own happiness. When we pursue a career in such a way that there is not sufficient time for meaningful relationships with God and neighbor, again we lose out, as do our families and our friends. When we love money so much that we will steal, lie, cheat, and fail to give to charity, we hurt not only others but also ourselves. Even though we rightly own our possessions, the use of everything we have, including our money, should be governed by love of God and neighbor.

Because God loves us deeply and wants us to be happy in this life and in the next, Jesus taught much about the disordered love of money: "No one can serve two masters; for either he will hate the one and love the other, or he will be devoted to the one and despise the other. You cannot serve God and mammon" (Mt 6:24). Mammon, the biblical false god of greed, drives people away from fellowship with each other and with God. In proclaiming these aspects of the Gospel, the Church serves human happiness.

Jesus also spoke of the great difficulty that the rich have of entering heaven: "Truly, I say to you, it will be hard for a rich man to enter the kingdom of heaven. Again I tell you, it is easier for a camel to go through the eye of a needle than for a rich man to enter the kingdom of God" (Mt 19:23–24). Commenting on this passage, Saint John Chrysostom writes: "What he spoke was not condemning riches in themselves, but those who were enslaved by them." [13] (It is easy to become a slave

---

[13] John Chrysostom, *Homilies on Matthew*, found in Thomas Aquinas, *Catena Aurea: Commentary on the Four Gospels, Collected Out of the Works of the Fathers*, vol. 1, pt. 2, *Gospel of St. Matthew* (New York: Cosimo Classics, 2007), p. 669.

to money, to devote one's life to the acquisition or purchase of material goods, but financial well-being is also a tool that can be used for good.)

The Church, therefore, calls all Christians to a spirit of detachment from worldly goods and riches. Our financial bottom line should not be the bottom line of our lives, our sole guide to behavior. A "spirit of poverty" should be sought by all Christians whereby they *use* worldly goods, including money, as tools for serving their neighbors. As Pope Benedict XVI points out, "Anyone who needs me, and whom I can help, is my neighbor." [14]

"Greed is good", said Gordon Gecko in the movie *Wall Street*. "Good for whom?" we might ask. Is it good for children who seldom see their father? Is it good for spouses so occupied with work that they have little time for each other? Is it good for those taken advantage of by financial misdeeds? We may not worship a golden statue in the desert, but most of us have to struggle against avarice, a grave impediment to our own happiness and the happiness of others. We tend to forget that God loves us, not only more than we love anyone else, but more than we love ourselves. Because of his great love for us, God urges us—and the Church echoes this warning—to avoid the worship of golden gods.

Again, there is nothing inherently wrong with money, or worldly success or bodily pleasures such as eating. Rather, the trouble comes when we think that these are the ultimate goals of life or when we seek level one or

[14] Pope Benedict XVI, *Deus Caritas Est* (*God Is Love*), December 25, 2005, no. 15.

level two in such a way that levels three or four are undermined. Undermining the higher levels of happiness in favor of the lower is inherently unreasonable. Even if we had all the money, fame, and power in the world, all the bodily pleasure we could handle, and all the worldly success possible, we could not be happy without true friendship and true love.

The Church continually proposes that human happiness consists in love and that level-three and level-four happiness—love for neighbor and love for God—go together. The two great commandments given by Jesus make this clear: "You shall love the Lord your God with all your heart, and with all your soul, and with all your mind. . . . You shall love your neighbor as yourself" (Mt 22:37, 39). If we truly love God, we will also love people, for they are made in his image and likeness. We cannot truly love God without also loving our neighbor. Indeed, the teachings of Jesus point us toward higher levels of happiness by guiding us toward this love: "A new commandment I give to you, that you love one another; even as I have loved you" (Jn 13:34). Sin, as Augustine pointed out, is nothing other than disordered love, a disordered love that robs us of happiness.[15] Happiness ultimately consists in rightly ordered love—love primarily for God and love for our neighbor, and only in a lesser place love for lesser things. We can have all the booze, drugs, sex, money, and power in the world—the life of the celebrity—but without love we will still not be happy.

[15] Augustine of Hippo, *De moribus ecclesiae catholicae et de moribus Manichaeorum* (Schoeningh Ferdinand GmbH, 2003).

The Church therefore invites all people to a life of love and service—the life of a saint.

Which way ultimately leads to happiness? The way of the celebrity or the way of the saint? Considering history, I am not sure how much more evidence can be gathered that the life of the celebrity does not guarantee happiness. How many of those who have more fame, money, alcohol, sex, power, and prestige than virtually everyone have been so deliriously happy that they have ended their lives in suicide? No one who is happy commits the ultimate act of misery. Celebrities ancient and contemporary bear testimony that even superabundant money, pleasure, power, and fame cannot satisfy the human heart's search for true happiness. By contrast, every saint experiences and exhibits joy—no saint is canonized without it. This joy usually exists simultaneously with hardship and sacrificial service, but it is a deep, pervasive, and lasting joy nonetheless. The Church, therefore, does not oppose true happiness, but rather only opposes a false conception of happiness that makes a god out of riches, fame, power, or pleasure. These false gods cannot provide true and lasting happiness. Those who worship them end in tears.

All the prohibitions taught by the Church—all the times the Church says no—are in the service to an overriding yes to love for God and neighbor. Consider the Ten Commandments. They are nothing but various ways in which we are commanded to love God or love our neighbor. If we worship false gods, if we dishonor God's name, if we do not make time to worship God on the Sabbath, then we fail to love him properly. If we dishonor our parents, if we murder, commit adultery, steal, bear false witness, and harbor covetous desires toward what belongs to our neighbor, then we fail to love our neighbor properly. Each "Thou Shall Not" is a way of saying yes to love for God or neighbor—the way to true happiness.

Commenting on Aristotle, who argued that human happiness necessarily involves friendship, Saint Thomas Aquinas added that we can be friends, not only with other human creatures, but also with God. Psychological research confirms this ancient wisdom. The happiest people have meaningful work that serves others (activity in accordance with virtue), and they have strong, loving relationships with their family, friends, and God. It turns out that in helping so many people to escape poverty, the Catholic Church also fosters *meaningful activity* (level-three happiness) among her members and those non-Catholics who cooperate in the Catholic institutional ventures in education, health care, and relief services for the needy, mentioned above. Few activities are more meaningful and significant than teaching, healing, and caring for those in need.

The Church's primary mission, however, is not simply level-three happiness, but rather level-four happiness. The Church exists to carry on the mission of Jesus, which is to reconcile all people to God the Father. The Church is not primarily a social-service organization; she is rather a religious family filled with adopted children of God. This spiritual emphasis itself contributes to people's happiness. On average, psychologists have found that people who practice their faith report greater happiness than those who do not. "According to a Gallup survey, the closer people feel to God, the better they feel about themselves and other people. One of the most comprehensive social surveys found that more than 48 percent of adults who are both married and weekly churchgoers reported that they are very happy, compared to just 20 percent of unmarried adults who don't attend church." Similarly, evidence collated by Pat Fagan of the Marriage and Religion Institute found that religious involvement is associated with feelings of well-being, positive moods, and greater satisfaction with sex, marriage, work, and life in general. Religious involvement is also associated with mental health. It goes along with lower rates of depression, suicide, drug and alcohol abuse, delinquency among teenagers, recidivism in adult criminals, and divorce rates.[16]

Some psychologists attribute these benefits to belonging to a community, and there certainly are benefits to communal belonging. But it is also true that the central teachings of Jesus, echoed liturgically by the Church each day in worship, themselves facilitate happiness. Take, for instance, forgiveness. Forgiveness is the trait most strongly linked to happiness, according to University of Michigan psychologist Christopher Peterson. Those who forgive let go of their resentments, cease mulling over pain and hurt, and therefore live fuller and happier lives. Of course, the teachings of Jesus emphasize, repeatedly, the importance of forgiveness, even for enemies. "Then Peter came up and said to him, 'Lord, how often shall my brother sin against me, and I forgive him? As many as seven times?'

[16] See Patrick Fagan and Althea Nagai, "The Benefit of Religious Attendance: Positive Outcomes Associated with Weekly Worship", http://downloads.frc.org/EF/EF11L30.pdf.

Jesus said to him, 'I do not say to you seven times, but seventy times seven'" (Mt 18:21–22). Through the proclamation of the Gospel, this message continues to resound. At each Mass, Catholics pray the words given by Jesus, "Forgive us our trespasses, as we forgive those who trespass against us." This emphasis on forgiveness aids human happiness.

Contemporary psychologists also emphasize the importance of optimism for happiness. Suffering, pain, and loss are a part of every human life. We experience minor setbacks and major ones. Consider, for example, those who suffered in concentration camps: physically abused, daily threatened by murderous death, enduring the loss of all property and privacy, and mourning the extinction of so many friends and relatives. In his book *Man's Search for Meaning*, Viktor Frankl pointed out that people in these horrible circumstances nevertheless reacted in radically different ways. Some killed themselves; others praised God even as they walked into the gas chambers. As Frankl remarked, "He who has a *why* to live for can bear with almost any *how*." [17] Things go wrong for everyone, but optimistic people believe that the setback is not permanent nor pervasive. By contrast, pessimistic people view upsetting situations as lasting forever and ruining everything. Not surprisingly, people with optimistic beliefs are happier than people with pessimistic beliefs.

The Christian virtue of hope bolsters an optimistic rather than a pessimistic perspective. The *Catechism of the*

---

[17] Viktor Frankl, *Man's Search for Meaning* (Boston: Beacon Press, 2000), p. 84.

Catholic Church defines hope as "the theological virtue by which we desire the kingdom of heaven and eternal life as our happiness, placing our trust in Christ's promises and relying not on our own strength, but on the help of the grace of the Holy Spirit" (no. 1817). Christians enjoying the virtue of hope can have confidence that no matter how badly things may be going, the present suffering will not last forever nor ruin everything, because, with God's help, perfect happiness is attainable in the life to come.

In his second encyclical letter, *Spe Salvi*, Pope Benedict XVI emphasizes the indispensability of hope for those who encounter suffering of whatever depth: "[T]he present, even if it is arduous, can be lived and accepted if it leads towards a goal, if we can be sure of this goal, and if this goal is great enough to justify the effort of the journey."[18] Despite all the difficulties of life, Christians never need to fear the future. Pope Benedict writes: "We see as a distinguishing mark of Christians the fact that they have a future: It is not that they know the details of what awaits them, but they know in general terms that their life will not end in emptiness. Only when the future is certain as a positive reality does it become possible to live the present as well" (no. 2). Man needs hope, not only for the future, but also for the present. Infused with hope, men can endure even the worst of circumstances. In proclaiming the possibility of perfect happiness in heaven, the Church facilitates even happiness on earth.

---

[18] Pope Benedict XVI, *Spe Salvi* (*Saved by Hope*), November 30, 2007, no. 1.

One final way in which the spiritual practice of the Church facilitates happiness is her emphasis on gratitude and thanksgiving. Psychologists have found that those who are grateful and practice giving thanks to others have significantly higher levels of happiness than those who do not. They have studied a practice, called the "Three Good Things" exercise, and found that it significantly increases happiness by making us more aware of what gives us joy.[19]

The practice is simple. First, at the end of each day, write down three positive things, large or small, that you experienced. They could relate to any of the four levels of happiness. (I had a really good cheeseburger; I finally got that promotion; I helped my son with his math homework; I felt close to God in prayer.) Those who undertake this practice report that they are significantly happier than those who did not.

Saint Ignatius Loyola discovered this secret centuries ago in his daily Jesuit "examen", which begins by recognizing the blessings God has given that day. The practice of thanksgiving is deeply rooted in Scripture: "Always and for everything giving thanks ... to God" (Eph 5:20). Thanksgiving Day comes only once a year for most people, but the celebration of each Mass or Eucharist—which literally means "thanksgiving" in Greek—is a standing invitation to thank God for the blessings of our lives. These religious practices facilitate deeper happiness among those who practice them.

In sum, the Catholic Church facilitates happiness in not only the social services that she sponsors but most

[19] Lyubomirsky, *The How of Happiness*, p. 15.

especially in her specifically religious practices, such as worship. Even if it is admitted that the Church facilitates happiness, many might still believe that the Church opposes freedom. But what exactly is *freedom*?

Again, there are rival conceptions. One understanding of freedom is simply the power to be able to do whatever we want, when we want, and how we want. In this sense, freedom is similar to personal control over a situation, a great contributor to happiness. The late, great Dominican theologian Servais Pinckaers described this as "freedom of indifference". He contrasted freedom of indifference with "freedom for excellence", the power to be able to perform excellent actions, actions that embody love for God and love for neighbor. The difference between the two kinds of freedom is similar to the difference between a novice and an expert piano player. A person completely lacking musical training who has working fingers has "freedom of indifference" to hit any note on the piano, but only a skilled pianist has not only freedom of indifference but also the "freedom for excellence" to be able to play a beautiful and complex song on the piano to entertain friends. This analogy is imperfect, for playing the piano is a mere skill that can be used for good or evil purposes, whereas freedom for excellence is the power to perform only good acts, the power to love.

The Church does not oppose *either* freedom of indifference *or* freedom for excellence. God made people with freedom of indifference, the choice to do good or to do evil. This freedom for people to make choices is itself good in that it allows for the existence of love. Freedom of the will makes possible true friendship and true character. God could have chosen to reign over a kingdom of chemicals in which merely material beings did whatever the laws of nature compelled them to do. However, he chose instead to create some beings that are free. We are free to love, and therefore are also free not to love. Freedom of indifference is a means, a necessary condition for the deeper and more significant kind of freedom, freedom for excellence.

It is true that in premodern societies throughout the world, the power of religion and the power of the state were often intertwined so that violations of theological orthodoxy were often viewed as also treasonable offenses against the government. Prior to a full differentiation between religious authority and state authority, it was difficult, if not impossible, properly to differentiate actions that are rightly considered crimes against the common good of civil society on the one hand, and violations of the ecclesial good on the other. However, it was the Catholic Church that initiated the differentiation between the proper roles of Church and state. The interplay between these two entities is complex. Historian Robert Louis Wilken points out:

> For centuries, the European states had been more eager to manage the affairs of the Church than the Church had been to intrude in civil matters. Moreover, the very notion that Church and state were two independent realms, one secular and one spiritual, was a consequence of the revolution inaugurated by Gregory VII [d. 1085] eight hundred years earlier. . . . Something genuinely novel did come out of the medieval conflict between pope and king, and the initiative

came from the Church's leaders and thinkers, not Europe's temporal rulers. Gregory VII was the bearer of a tradition that reached back to the gospels ("Then render to Caesar the things that are Caesar's, and to God the things that are God's"), to Ambrose and Augustine, and to Pope Gelasius, who said that the "two principles" that give order to the world—political authority and spiritual authority—were distinct. This was the gift of the West.[20]

In earlier as well as contemporary times, the Church defended personal control over one's life. In premodern times, the Church defended the necessity of free consent in marriage against manipulation and control over marriage by powerful families. The Church defended the freedom to choose not to marry, as well as the freedom not to be forced into an arranged marriage without consent, even for those who were "slaves" in the premodern sense of the term.[21] In modern times, the Church embraced freedom of indifference, for example, by opposing communists and Nazi totalitarian governments, which removed certain fundamental freedoms such as religious liberty and private property from their citizens. Indeed, outside of enforcing local legal regulations in Vatican City, the Church has no power whatsoever to "enforce" her views about anything with criminal penalties such as fines or imprisonment. The Church cannot "take away" anyone's freedom, nor does she want to. In the words of Pope Benedict, "We impose nothing, yet we propose

[20] Robert Louis Wilken, "The Gift of the West", *First Things: A Monthly Journal of Religion & Public Life*, 200 (February 2010): 52–53. *Academic Search Complete*, EBSCO*host* (accessed September 28, 2010).

[21] Thomas Aquinas, *Summa Theologiae*, Supplement: 52:2.

ceaselessly. . . ."[22] The Church's appeal is to the conscience of all people of good will; the Church's proposal is that everyone lives a life worthy of human dignity and conducive to authentic human happiness.

However, as good as freedom of indifference is, there is a higher kind of freedom, freedom for excellence, true freedom, that alone can secure happiness. In the words of Pope Benedict XVI,

> [t]he Gospel teaches us that true freedom, the freedom of the children of God, is found only in the self-surrender which is part of the mystery of love. Only by losing ourselves, the Lord tells us, do we truly find ourselves (cf. Lk 17:33). True freedom blossoms when we turn away from the burden of sin, which clouds our perceptions and weakens our resolve, and find the source of our ultimate happiness in him who is infinite love, infinite freedom, infinite life.[23]

The proclamation of true freedom is inextricably linked with the message and person of Jesus. True freedom is loving God and loving neighbor and thereby finding happiness in this life as well as in the life to come.

There is, however, a third kind of freedom that the Church does oppose—false freedom. False freedom is any choice that contradicts true freedom for excellence. The freedom of the drug addict taking heroin, the freedom

---

[22] Pope Benedict XVI, Homily, Av. dos Aliados Square, Porto, Portugal (May 14, 2010), http://www.vatican.va/holy_father/benedict_xvi/homilies/2010/documents/hf_ben-xvi_hom_20100514_porto_en.html.

[23] Pope Benedict XVI, Homily in Yankee Stadium, Bronx, New York, Fifth Sunday of Easter (April 20, 2008), http://www.vatican.va/holy_father/benedict_xvi/homilies/2008/documents/hf_ben-xvi_hom_20080420_yankee-stadium-ny_en.html.

of the killer mutilating his victim, and the freedom of the mother ruining her relationship with her child are each examples of false freedom, which destroys true happiness by rejecting proper love for God or for neighbor. Every sin manifests a lack of proper love for God, neighbor, or self, and so every sin is an act of false freedom. Since every sin undermines true happiness, the Church does stand in opposition to false freedom. She opposes false freedom not with fines, imprisonment, or force, but rather with an invitation to a change of heart and the opportunity for confession and reconciliation with God and others. Anyone who loves other people should stand in union with the Church against false freedom, for false freedom undermines the good of the human person by taking away happiness in this life and the next.

Without knowledge, we cannot be free. Without knowing the truth and acting in accordance with it, we cannot be truly free. Indeed, the Church's goal is to help us grow in freedom for excellence so that we can attain greater happiness in this life, and perfect happiness in the next. Thus, the Church extends the mission of Jesus, "If you continue in my word, you are truly my disciples, and you will know the truth, and the truth will make you free" (Jn 8:31–32). Helping us achieve our true happiness—both here and eternally—is the very mission of Jesus: "I came that they may have life, and have it abundantly" (Jn 10:10).

The Third Big Myth

The Church Hates Women: The Myth of Catholic Misogyny

The Catholic Church is subjected to a great deal of suspicion, if not outright scorn, when it comes to her treatment of women. Does the Church treat women as "second class"? In short, does the Catholic Church hate women? Few people would put the question that strongly, yet many believe the answer is yes.

As evidence, they point to sexist quotations from Church Fathers and sexist interpretations of Scripture. Even Scripture contains "subordination" passages, such as "let wives also be subject in everything to their husbands" (Eph 5:24). Moreover, the Catholic Church is also well-known for her opposition to abortion and contraception, which many believe are the keys to women's sexual and economic freedom. Finally, only men can be ordained priests. Isn't that clear evidence of discrimination? As one slogan puts it: "If women are good enough to be baptized, why aren't they good enough to be ordained?"

I think it is important to begin considering these issues by turning to the foundation of Catholic Christianity:

the life and teachings of Jesus. Whether authentic Christianity accords with the dignity of women is, at least in part, a question of whether Christ himself accorded women dignity. Christ's interaction with women suggests that he had an entirely new perspective on the dignity of women in the time and culture in which he lived:

- The public ministry of Jesus and his first miracle at Cana began at the request of a woman, his Mother (Jn 2:1–11).

- Jesus healed many women of their spiritual and physical disabilities (Lk 8:1–3); he spoke kindly to and healed the woman suffering years of blood loss (Mk 5:24–34).

- Jesus saved the life of the woman caught in adultery, saying, "Let him who is without sin among you be the first to throw a stone at her" (Jn 8:7).

- Breaking the sexist and racial customs of his day, Jesus spoke with the Samaritan woman at the well, offering her "living water" (Jn 4:10).

The late Notre Dame theologian Catherine Mowry Lacugna wrote that Jesus revealed himself to women as Messiah, discussed theology with women, healed women, was anointed and wept over by women, was accompanied by women throughout his ministry, especially during the last hours of his life, and he appeared to his beloved friend Mary Magdalene after his death.[1] On a Catholic view,

---

[1] Catherine Mowry Lacugna, "Catholic Women as Ministers and Theologians", *America*, October 10, 1992, 244.

Jesus suffered and died for the salvation of all mankind, and his love knows no exceptions. If Jesus really is the Son of God, then his divine nature is incompatible with sins of any kind, including sins against the dignity of women. Jesus himself was in no way sexist, nor did his own actions and teachings discriminate against women in any way.

Unfortunately, members of the Church have not always followed Christ as closely as they should with respect to the treatment of women. As Pope John Paul II confessed, many members of the Church, including some in the hierarchy, have acted—and sometimes still act—in ways that fail to express the equality of man and woman. As John Paul wrote:

> And if objective blame [for offenses against the dignity of women], especially in particular historical contexts, has belonged to not just a few members of the Church, for this I am truly sorry. May this regret be transformed, on the part of the whole Church, into a renewed commitment of fidelity to the Gospel vision. When it comes to setting women free from every kind of exploitation and domination, the Gospel contains an ever relevant message that goes back to the *attitude of Jesus Christ himself*. Transcending the established norms of his own culture, Jesus treated women with openness, respect, acceptance, and tenderness. In this way he honored the dignity that women have always possessed according to God's plan and in his love. As we look to Christ at the end of this second millennium, it is natural to ask ourselves: How much of his message has been heard and acted upon?[2]

---

[2] Pope John Paul II, *Letter to Women* (June 29, 1995), no. 3.

The situation today is, one hopes, better than it once was, but sexual and physical abuse of women still occurs, as do unjust discrimination and the failure to recognize talents.

Of course, failing in Christian discipleship is not limited to wrongdoing against the dignity of women. Baptism does not remove the believer from temptations and weaknesses, nor does it guarantee appropriate behavior. Membership in the Church does not prevent a person from sinning against women, or against anyone else. Obviously, it is not only Catholics who victimize women, and it is not only women who are victimized. As Robert Burns wrote, "Man's inhumanity to man makes countless thousands mourn." [3] Cruel and unfeeling behavior stretches further back than Cain and Abel to Adam's blaming of Eve.

But such shortcomings do not reflect what the Church is called to be. Sins against young and old, black and white, male and female, are characteristic of all people— Catholic and non-Catholic alike. What is characteristic of Christians, though, is the imitation of Christ. The degree to which someone does not imitate Christ is the degree to which that person fails to be fully Christian. There is a long list of "Catholic" murderers. But when a Catholic commits murder, he separates himself from Christ, and therefore from the body of Christ, the Church. In like manner, whenever a Catholic acts against the dignity of women, he too separates himself from Christ and from Christ's Church.

---

[3] Robert Burns and James Currie, *The Works of Robert Burns*, vol. 3, 7th edition (Edinburgh: Black Horse Court, 1813), p. 186.

In addition to the sad but real failings of some Catholics to live up to their calling in their treatment of women, it is also correct that Christian theologians have sometimes fallen short in their estimation of women. Personal sin undoubtedly plays a role in the corruption of theology, but the cultural context must also be considered. Christianity arose in an environment of universally assumed female inequality. Greek philosophy and other sources of ancient thought are rife with misogynistic judgments. It is not surprising that the Church Fathers sometimes adopted these attitudes without critical reflection—and some academics have been quick to interpret passages in the least charitable light. John Paul II noted this in his *Letter to Women*:

> Unfortunately, we are heirs to a history that has conditioned us to a remarkable extent. In every time and place, this conditioning has been an obstacle to the progress of women. Women's dignity has often been unacknowledged and their prerogatives misrepresented; they have often been relegated to the margins of society and even reduced to servitude. This has prevented women from truly being themselves, and it has resulted in a spiritual impoverishment of humanity. Certainly it is no easy task to assign the blame for this, considering the many kinds of cultural conditioning that down the centuries have shaped ways of thinking and acting.[4]

Just as Christian thinkers will sometimes uncritically adopt the scientific outlook of the day, so, too, in the social realm. Hence, Fathers of the Church and great Scholastic doctors not only at times uncritically repeat the sexist

[4] Pope John Paul II, *Letter to Women* (June 29, 1995), no. 3.

truisms inherited from the secular culture of their day, but sometimes interpret the theological tradition in light of those assumptions. The same attitudes and judgments can also inform the reading of Scripture.

These theologians stand in need of correction. If revelation is really from God, then nothing revealed can be false or lacking in justice or goodness. But the same does not hold true for any individual's interpretation of revelation, even a saintly and learned individual. The development of doctrine leads to a greater understanding of revelation in part by sorting out what actually pertains to revelation from what only seems to.

For example, Saint Thomas Aquinas, following the sexist views of antiquity, held that the male sex is more noble than the female. At the same time, Aquinas believed that the female sex should not be despised on this account, since Christ took his flesh from a woman (*Summa Theologiae* III:31:4 ad 1). In other passages, too, Thomas shows an awareness of the equality of men and women recognized by Christ: "If a husband were permitted to abandon his wife, the society of husband and wife would not be an association of equals but, instead, a sort of slavery on the part of the wife" (*Summa contra Gentiles* III:124:[4]). In fact, Thomas used the idea of equality in marital friendship to argue in favor of an unconditional love between husband and wife:

> The greater the friendship is, the more solid and long lasting it will be. Now there seems to be the greatest friendship between husband and wife, for they are united not only in the act of fleshly union, which produces a certain gentle association even among beasts, but also in the partnership of

the whole range of domestic activity. Consequently, as an indication of this, man must even "leave his father and mother" for the sake of his wife as it is said in Genesis (2:24).[5]

Furthermore, Aquinas believed that the fact that Eve was made from Adam's rib indicates that she was not above him (as she might be had she been created from Adam's head) nor below him, like a slave (as she might be had she arisen from his feet). She comes from his side, indicating that she is a partner and companion. These statements of the equality of man and woman represent the new and distinctly Christian point of view, though in Thomas as in many patristic writers, the preexisting pagan attitude is not entirely shaken off. It has taken some time for the wheat to be separated from the chaff.

Indeed, when you look at the writings of Enlightenment figures, such as Arthur Schopenhauer, who self-consciously sought to distance themselves from what they took to be distinctly Christian ideas, you find a recurrence of the ancient attitudes of disrespect for women. Schopenhauer writes:

> Women, taken as a whole, are and remain thorough and incurable philistines: so that, with the extremely absurd arrangement by which they share the rank and title of their husband, they are a continual spur to his *ignoble* ambitions. They are *sexus sequior*, the inferior second sex in *every* respect: one should be indulgent toward their weaknesses, but to pay them honour is ridiculous beyond measure and demeans us even in their eyes. This is how the peoples of antiquity and of the Orient have regarded women; they have recognized what is

---

[5] Thomas Aquinas, *Summa contra Gentiles*, book 3, part II, trans. Vernon Bourke (Notre Dame: University of Notre Dame Press, 1991), ch. 123, p. 148.

the proper position for women far better than we have, we
with our Old French gallantry and insipid women-veneration,
that highest flower of Christian-Germanic stupidity.[6]

Put differently, those cultures unaffected by Christian
belief—the ancient pagan world, the Orient, and we might
add Islamic countries—do not accord women the same
status as do countries such as France and Germany, who
were deeply influenced by Christian ideas about the fundamental equality between men and women, husband and
wife. This influence is prevalent even today in cultures
deeply influenced by Catholicism, such as Central America and South America, where preference for male children is weaker than in other areas of the world.[7]

The fundamental equality of all people is reflected in
Christian moral codes that hold men and women to the
same standards of behavior. Again, the idea that there
should be one moral code that applies equally to both
sexes is an innovation of Christian belief. At the time
of Christ, Mosaic law allowed a husband to leave his
wife, but a wife could not leave her husband. Jesus' teaching leveled the playing field by calling both husband and
wife to be faithful to their vows of love "until death do
us part": "Whoever divorces his wife and marries another,
commits adultery against her; and if she divorces her
husband and marries another, she commits adultery"
(Mk 10:11–12). The prohibition of divorce established

---

[6] Arthur Schopenhauer, *Essays and Aphorisms*, trans. R. J. Hollingdale (London: Penguin Classics, 1970), p. 86.

[7] Mary Anne Warren, "Sex Selection: Individual Choice or Cultural Coer-
cion?" in *Bioethics: An Anthology*, ed. Helga Kuhse and Peter Singer (Oxford:
Blackwell Publishers, 1999), pp. 137–42, at 139.

Christianity as the only religion in the history of the world to call its members to strict monogamy. This teaching of Jesus protected women, who, especially in the ancient world, were typically put at tremendous economic and social disadvantage in cases of divorce. The Catholic Church also fought for a view of marriage that involved the consent of both the man and the woman in opposition to powerful cultural forces that viewed arranged marriage without consent as the norm. In addition, the Church championed the idea that women need not consent to marriage at all, but are free to remain single.

In Christian ethics, men and women are subject to the same moral standards also in terms of sexual behavior. This too differs from the ancient way of condoning male promiscuity but condemning the same behavior for women, or the post-Christian habit of celebrating men as "studs" while condemning women as "sluts". Church Father Gregory of Nazianzus writes:

> The majority of men are ill-disposed to chastity and their laws are unequal and irregular. For what was the reason they restrained the woman but indulged the man, and that a woman who practices evil against her husband's bed is an adulteress and the penalties of the law severe, but if the husband commits fornication against his wife, he has no account to give? I do not accept this legislation. I do not approve this custom. (*Oration* 37:6)

By establishing one moral code obligatory on men and women alike,[8] Christianity fostered a lasting commitment

[8] See too, St. Jerome, Letter 77 and St. Ambrose, *De Abraham* 1,4.

of unconditional covenantal love, protecting the family structure and putting the sexes on an equal footing.

Christian morality offered a refreshing perspective to
women in the ancient world accustomed to husbands who
cheated and left at will. The number of women who con-
verted to Christianity in the early centuries after Christ indicates that women were attracted to this new way of life.
Indeed, they were among the most zealous converts and
defenders of the faith. As historian Henry Chadwick notes,

> Christianity seems to have been especially successful among
> women. It was often through the wives that it penetrated the
> upper classes of society in the first instance. Christians believed
> in the equality of men and women before God and found in
> the New Testament commands that husbands should treat
> their wives with such consideration and love as Christ man-
> ifested for his Church. Christian teaching about the sanctity
> of marriage offered a powerful safeguard to married women.[9]

Throughout the history of the Church, this pattern
has held true. There are more women converts and more
women active in the life of the Church than men. Catherine Lacugna, writing about our time, notes:

> Over 85 percent of those responsible for altar preparation
> are women. Over 80 percent of CCD teachers and spon-
> sors for the catechumenate are women. Over 75 percent of
> adult Bible study leaders and participants are women. Over
> 70 percent of those active in parish renewal and spiritual
> growth are women, and over 80 percent of those who join
> prayer groups are women. Nearly 60 percent of those involved
> with youth groups and recreational activities are women.
> Over 85 percent of those who lead or assist in ministries

[9] Henry Chadwick, *The Early Church* (London: Penguin, 1993), pp. 58–59.

designed to help the poor, visit the sick, comfort the grieving, and minister to the handicapped are women.[10]

At Mass on any given Sunday, chances are that there will be many more women than men. The sheer number of women so dedicated to the Church over the course of two millennia is difficult to reconcile with the idea of a pervasively misogynistic Church—unless one assumes the patronizing idea that these women are uneducated, confused, or deeply disturbed.

Is it fair to say that women participating in the institutional Church are uneducated, confused, or deeply disturbed? Demographic information about the kinds of women active in the life of the Church makes this charge impossible to sustain. Lacugna notes that the typical Catholic woman engaged in ministry is married with children, usually between thirty-six and forty-nine years of age, middle class, and well educated—not exactly the typical profile of an unhinged, ignorant person. Indeed, some of these women in service to the Church are among the intellectual elite, such as Mary Ann Glendon, the Learned Hand Professor of Law at Harvard University; Elizabeth Fox-Genovese, the Eléonore Raoul Professor of the Humanities at Emory University; Helen Alvare, Professor of Law at George Mason University; and the world-renowned University of Cambridge philosopher Elizabeth Anscombe. If the Catholic Church were pervasively misogynistic, it is impossible to imagine that such intelligent, accomplished modern women would remain members, let alone dedicate their services to the institution.

[10] Lacugna, "Catholic Women as Ministers and Theologians" 240.

Compare this situation with the number of African-Americans working for the KKK, and it becomes clear how distant—indeed light years apart—is the Catholic Church from a truly discriminatory and hateful institution.

But what should be made of the subordination passages in Scripture, such as "let wives also be subject in everything to their husbands" (Eph 5:24)? This passage appears to contradict the idea that Christianity views the sexes as equal.

This and similar passages *have* sometimes been used to justify unfair treatment toward women. Indeed, Scripture can be twisted to justify things that are very much opposed to the message of Jesus. Imagine I flip open a Bible at random and read, "[H]e [Judas] went and hanged himself" (Mt 27:5), and then, "Go and do likewise" (Lk 10:37). This obviously is not a good interpretation of Scripture.

The Catholic tradition holds that individual passages in the Bible should be read in a way that accords with the overall message of the Gospel. Saint Augustine, in his book *On Christian Doctrine*, said that Scripture can be rightly interpreted in a variety of ways, but that any understanding of a passage that undermined love of God or love of neighbor ought to be rejected. For Catholics, we distinguish false from good readings of Scripture in part by making use of the guidance of the Magisterium, the official teachings of the Church, such as the teachings of popes. Fortunately, Pope John Paul II commented explicitly on the passage in question. He writes: "The author knows that this way of speaking, so profoundly rooted in the customs and religious traditions of the time, is to be understood and carried out in a new way: as a 'mutual subjection out of reverence for Christ'.... The woman cannot be made the object of domination and male possession."[11] That husband and wife are to be subject to one another is reinforced in the next verse of the original passage cited: "Husbands, love your wives, as Christ loved the Church and gave himself up for her" (Eph 5:25). This injunction to love transforms the potentially selfish orientation of male love into a form of intense self-sacrificial service. Subordination is mutual, but the admonition to love as Christ loves is given to husbands in particular, perhaps because they need it more. What is implied, then, is not general female inferiority but, if anything, a general female superiority in the order that most matters in the end—the order of charity. It is true that the subordination passage could be used to argue for the inferiority of women, but in the Catholic understanding proposed by Pope John Paul II this would be a serious misunderstanding and twisting of the proper meaning of the passage.

The reservation of priestly ordination to men is perhaps the sorest spot among contemporary critics of the Catholic Church's treatment of women. Many people understandably believe that the Church feels that women are less holy, less intellectually capable, less pastorally sensitive, or less capable of leadership than men. It is true that some medieval theologians defended male priestly ordination with just such arguments.

---

[11] Pope John Paul II, *Mulieris Dignitatem* (*On the Dignity and Vocation of Women*, August 15, 1988), nos. 24, 10.

In order to understand better this controversial question, it is again important to return to the example of Jesus. As noted earlier, the behavior, teaching, and attitude of Jesus toward women (and everyone else) exemplifies a model of what all people of good will should strive to embody in their own lives. Catholics believe that Jesus loved us enough to want to be with us, not only in his words recorded in Scripture, not only in the Church community who gathers to remember and celebrate Jesus' life, but also in the sacraments, outward signs instituted by Christ to give us a share in his divine life. The seven sacraments—baptism, confession, Holy Communion, confirmation, marriage, anointing of the sick, and holy orders, in a Catholic view, are given by Christ himself. Since Jesus has established these sacraments himself, no one—including the pope and bishops—is free to add new sacraments, though we can pray in various other ways, nor is anyone free to abolish sacraments. Jesus himself established the sacraments, and the Church, in obedience to the Lord, is free only to follow what Christ has established.

The sacrament of baptism, for example, must make use of water and not sand. This does not imply that sand is less important or valuable than water; indeed, those lost at sea need an island of sand much more than they need water. Similarly, the sacrament of anointing of the sick makes use of holy oils rather than bread or wine, even though bread and wine—or at least food of some kind—is much more important to human survival than is oil for anointing. In like manner, the Eucharist must make use of bread and wine, even in cultural contexts like Germany, where presumably many celebrating the Eucharist would prefer a meal of sausage and beer. Similarly, the Church teaches that Christ established that the proper recipient of the sacrament of holy orders is a baptized male. Jesus—though sinless and the perfect exemplar of love toward all—did not include any women among the twelve apostles. As Joseph Cardinal Ratzinger noted before his election as Pope Benedict XVI: "One forgets that in the ancient world all religions also had priestesses. All except one: the Jewish. Christianity, here too following the 'scandalous' original example of Jesus, opens a new situation to women; it accords them a position that represents a novelty with respect to Judaism. But of the latter he preserves the exclusively male priesthood." [12] Jesus, of course, broke with Jewish custom in numerous ways, but here he retained it. Just as Christ's selection of only men to be his apostles did not exhibit or imply in any way the inferiority of women, so too the continuation of this particular apostolic ministry by men does not manifest the belief that women are inferior.

The alternative is to label Jesus himself sexist, when just the opposite is true. It is no coincidence that the heretical groups called Macrionites and Gnostics, who rejected the Old Testament but accepted the New Testament, also introduced female priests. But one should not, however, suppose that these groups had a high regard for women. They believed that the salvation of women

---

[12] Joseph Cardinal Ratzinger, *The Ratzinger Report* (San Francisco: Ignatius Press, 1985), p. 94.

was in making themselves as much as possible like men. Hence the Gnostic Gospel of Thomas says, "A woman who makes herself a man will enter the kingdom of heaven." The whole life and teaching of Jesus, including his calling of the Twelve, indicates another view, one that affirms both the male priesthood and the value of women as women, not mere imitators of men. The Church has no authority to reduce or increase the number of sacraments, nor the authority to change the matter that is used in a sacrament, nor the authority to deny the intrinsic dignity of all people, male and female alike.

But if Jesus chose twelve men to be the first priests, and indicated by his choice that priesthood should be reserved for men, why not also conclude that only men of Jewish origin should be priests? After all, the twelve apostles were all Jewish. If we can extend the priesthood also to Gentiles, by like reasoning the priesthood should also include women.

This objection does not succeed, for several reasons. In a sense, the apostles were no longer Jewish, since they had begun to put their trust in Christ in such a way that his teaching and practice took precedence over Jewish teaching and practice (cf. Mt 12:1–8). Secondly, the Old Testament prophesies about a time when the priesthood would not be tied to one's genetic background or genealogy as was the Jewish priesthood (cf. Gen 14:18–20; Ps 110:4). This prophecy came to fulfillment in the priesthood of Jesus, which is shared by the apostles and their successors and not linked to genetic background and family tree (cf. Heb 7:14–27). Finally, Dr. Manfred Hauke notes:

The widening of office [of the priesthood] is already implicitly contained in Jesus' missionary commandment, which initiates the program of extending the Church to all peoples. Therefore, there was never any controversy about the pros and cons of admitting Gentile Christians to apostolic office but only about the question of observance of certain Jewish customs by new members.[13]

Finally, women were among the earliest and most courageous followers of Jesus, yet he did not call them to be among the Twelve. Even his own Mother, who according to Catholic belief is the greatest human person in all of history, was not among the Twelve. Gentiles, by contrast, were not part of Jesus' early ministry. So it is not surprising that none of the Twelve were Gentiles, but it is significant that none of the Twelve were women.

This is not to say that women did not function or do not still function in ways associated with the priestly ministry. Women did and still do teach converts (Acts 18:26), have liturgical responsibilities (Rom 16:1), and act as prophets (1 Cor 11:5) and co-workers with the apostles (Phil 4:3). As noted earlier, these services provided by women in service to their fellow believers as well as to the wider community continue to the present day.

Why did Jesus choose twelve men to serve as apostles? Some theologians have even speculated that perhaps the reservation of priestly orders to males reflects not male superiority but male inferiority, namely, that men are typically worse people than women. Most murderers, rapists,

[13] Manfred Hauke, *Women in the Priesthood: A Systematic Analysis in the Light of the Order of Creation and Redemption* (San Francisco: Ignatius Press, 1988), p. 334.

thieves, and scoundrels of the highest order are men. It is, therefore, men and not women who are in particular need of models of self-sacrificial service and love. A priest is one who gives sacrifice, and the sacrifice is not only something he does but something he is. Fulton J. Sheen wrote:

> We who have received the sacrament of orders call ourselves "priests." The author does not recall any priest ever having said that "I was ordained a victim." And yet, was not Christ the Priest, a Victim? Did he not come to die? He did not offer a lamb, a bullock, or doves; he never offered anything except himself. "He gave himself up on our behalf, a sacrifice breathing out a fragrance as he offered it to God" (Eph. 5:2). . . . So we have a mutilated concept of our priesthood if we envisage it apart from making ourselves victims in the prolongation of his Incarnation.[14]

The priesthood is misconstrued in terms of domination, power, and exultation; it is properly understood in terms of service, love, and sacrifice, and there are more than enough opportunities for both men and women to exercise these offices outside of the priesthood.

Bishop Elden F. Curtiss considers the issue of women's ordination from another perspective:

> Could the role of Hamlet in Shakespeare's famous drama be portrayed adequately by a woman as a woman? Only if the plot were rewritten and the relationships and the dialogue of the main characters substantially changed, but then it would not be the work of Shakespeare. Whereas Hamlet's fictitious life merely is recalled with each celebration of the play, in the Eucharistic celebration the life, death, and

[14] Fulton J. Sheen, *The Priest Is Not His Own* (New York, Toronto, London: McGraw-Hill, 1963), p. 2.

resurrection of Jesus is re-presented in its present reality. It would be, therefore, even less appropriate for a woman to portray the role of Jesus in the Eucharist than to portray the role of Hamlet in the play. Jesus was not born a woman, and He should not be portrayed as a woman in the reenactment of his suffering and death as a man.[15]

To use a different example, if we were to stage a Christmas pageant, rather than celebrate a Mass, no one would choose a man dressed as a man to play the role of Mary. Even less should a woman have the role of Jesus in the eucharistic celebration.

It is almost always assumed by advocates of women's ordination that the "full and active participation" in the Church called for by the Second Vatican Council (*Sacrosanctum Concilium*, no. 14) requires priestly ordination. The view that only priests are called to holiness or to important roles or to "full and active" participation in the Church is often called clericalism, an idea rejected by the Council. The layperson can participate actively and fully in the Church—as a layperson. The Spirit bestows different gifts on different people. As the First Letter to the Corinthians indicates, just as the human body has different members and each member a different purpose, so, too, the various parts of the body of Christ—successors to the apostles, prophets, teachers, healers, helpers, administrators—are all essential, valuable, and vital (cf. 1 Cor 12:4–30). The clericalist view implies that Mother Teresa, Saint Thomas More, Saint Francis of Assisi, and the Virgin Mary did not fully

[15] Bishop Elden F. Curtiss, quoted in Christopher Kaczor, "Women in the Priesthood: An Ignatian Reconsideration of the Arguments", *Catholic Dossier* 1, no. 4 (1995): 21–28, at 24.

participate in the Church because they were not priests. Women have exercised and continue to exercise authority in the Church as presidents of Catholic universities, as chief administrators of hospitals, as chancellors of dioceses, and as CEOs of companies such as the Eternal Word Television Network (EWTN).

Of course, the ordination question can be explored at much greater length than I've addressed the issue here. But having read the literature extensively, I have also never read a critique of the Church's teaching that did not explicitly or implicitly rely on clericalist assumptions. More importantly, I know of no argument in any contemporary source defending the reservation of priestly ordination to men that invokes the idea that men are better, holier, smarter, more worthy, more pastorally sensitive, or superior in any talent to women.[16] The Catholic reservation of priestly ordination to men does not rest on misogyny.

The myth of Catholic misogyny is perhaps best addressed in terms of the practical care the Church offers to women (and men) throughout the world. Has any institution educated more women? Fed more women? Clothed more women? Rescued more female infants from death? Offered more assistance or medical care to mothers and their children? Fairness demands that not just the shortcomings of Catholics but also their successes be taken

---

[16] Interested readers should consult Hauke, *Women in the Priesthood*, mentioned above; Peter Kreeft and Alice von Hildebrand, *Women and the Priesthood* (Steubenville: Franciscan University Press, 1994); and Benedict Ashley, *Justice in the Church: Gender and Participation* (Washington, D.C.: The Catholic University of America Press, 1996).

into account in assessing the Church's stance toward women. I would argue that the Catholic Church has done more than any other single institution in the world to promote the well-being of women in providing food, shelter, clothing, health care, and education. For example, in 2008, in the United States alone, Catholic Charities served more than 8.5 million people, the majority of them women. In terms of education, the institutional U.S. Church educated 1,724,761 students at the grade-school level, 672,426 at the high-school level, and 785,619 at the college level, a majority of whom were female.[17] The time, resources, and money expended by the Catholic Church as an institution to improve the well-being of women is impossible to reconcile with the belief that the Church is "anti-woman". After all, a truly discriminatory organization spends no time, no money, and no effort whatsoever to improve the well-being of those that they hate. The Aryan Nation does not build schools to educate black people alongside white people.

Some members of the Church have undoubtedly behaved badly, but it is no less true that other members of the Church have behaved well—often heroically well— toward women. When they have done so, they have been even more fully incorporated into the mystical body of Christ, who came to serve, love, and save all people, and in whose image—as God—he created both male and female.

---

[17] United States Conference of Catholic Bishops, *Catholic Education in the United States at a Glance*, http://www.uspapalvisit.org/backgrounders/education.htm (accessed January 12, 2012).

The Fourth Big Myth

Indifferent to Love, the Church Banned Contraception: The Myth of Opposition between Love and Procreation

The Church's teaching on contraception is perhaps her most challenging and difficult, as well as her most maligned and misunderstood. Most people today, including most Catholics, view the use of contraception, "safe sex", as not only not wrong but in many cases a positive duty. Why in the world would anyone, for any reason, view contraception as problematic, let alone morally wrong?

Imagine a world in which almost no one understood the value of private property. In such a world, it would be nearly impossible to explain why stealing was wrong. Or imagine that virtually no one thought that telling the truth was important. In such a world, an ethical imperative not to lie would make no sense. To make sense of Catholic teaching on contraception, we must first reconsider the value of fertility and having children. Only in this perspective can one begin to understand what the Church teaches.

Is fertility a curse or a blessing? Is it a good thing or a bad thing to have children? Does procreation inhibit or foster our well-being? These questions can be considered from a variety of perspectives, but let us consider them from the perspective of erotic love, of friendship, and of eternal happiness in heaven.

Does Procreation Enhance or Thwart Marital Erotic Love?

To answer this question, we must first ask, "What exactly is erotic love?" It is important, I think, not just in this discussion but for many other issues as well, to distinguish *erotic love* from mere *sexual attraction* to someone. It can be hard, especially when experienced, to distinguish these two states of being, in particular, because they have much in common. Both erotic love and sexual attraction are outside of our control. We "fall in love" much like slipping on the ice or getting the hiccups. We cannot make ourselves not be in love if we are in love, and we cannot choose to fall in love with someone as we can choose to give them a hug or be nice to them. Similarly, when we encounter someone whom we find sexually attractive, we cannot help but find them attractive. There is something passive about both falling in love and being sexually attracted to someone; they happen to us sometimes without our conscious decision. Erotic love and sexual attraction are also alike in that they can be very intense, overwhelming, and exhilarating. Both can happen right away. Love at first sight as well as lust at first sight are common. Finally, both can be short-lived. We fall in love, but we can also fall out of love. We may find someone incredibly attractive at one time, but forty pounds later not so much. These similarities cause many people to confuse being in love with someone on the one hand and being sexually attracted to someone on the other.

But erotic love and mere sexual attraction are not exactly alike. One major difference is that those who are merely attracted wish for sexual union, but those who are in love yearn for sexual union and a lot more. They want to be united, not just sexually, but also in nonsexual terms. They want to spend time, not just in the bedroom, but also at work, at play, at rest, and in the everyday circumstances of life. Erotic love seeks a deep union in all matters, including those that are not at all sexual.

There is also an exclusivity to erotic love that is not shared by sexual attraction. Those who are in love yearn for the beloved alone. They seek only the one they love. By contrast, mere sexual attraction is satisfied by anyone equally attractive, indeed may find greater satisfaction in someone more attractive. The individual person is not so vitally important in sexual attraction, but is substitutable for anyone of like appearance or better. By contrast, erotic love views the beloved as unique, irreplaceable, and incapable of substitution.

Erotic love and sexual attraction also differ in terms of time as experienced. Erotic love has the air of eternity. When you are in love, you can hardly imagine not being in love. You can picture this experience continuing through the days, weeks, and months ahead into a glorious future. By contrast, mere sexual attraction is characterized by immediacy and urgency of the present moment. *I want her and I want her now* is the voice of mere sexual attraction. *I want her and I'll always want her* is the voice of erotic love.

Erotic love and mere sexual attraction are alike in causing preoccupation, but the preoccupation is importantly different in the two cases. Mere sexual attraction focuses exclusively on the person as a physical body, an actual or potential sexual partner. By contrast, erotic love focuses on the whole person. *I love the way she looks, but I also love the way she writes, her laugh, her humor, and her idiosyncrasies.* Erotic love accepts and glories in the whole person in her every aspect.

Finally, erotic love is centered on the beloved—what pleases her, what she wants, what I can do for her. By contrast, mere sexual attraction is more self-focused—what pleases me, what I want, what I can get from her. Self-sacrifice makes sense in terms of erotic love; self-sacrifice—without the thought of reward—does not make sense in terms of mere sexual attraction.

So, what difference does this make in terms of contraception? Although use of contraception makes perfect sense in terms of mere sexual attraction, contraception actually undermines, rather than accords with, the nature of erotic love. Erotic love—by its very nature—is a drive toward deeper unity with the beloved, and children are a wonderful manifestation of the unity between husband and wife.

Each child unifies the husband and wife with each other in a physical sense. Every one of us is a living manifestation of the union of our mother and father, half of our DNA from each. This unity, like erotic love itself, is the *exclusive* bringing together of one man and one woman.

No other woman is the mother of his child; no other man is the father of her child. As long as the child lives, they are unified in their offspring.

This unity is characteristically not limited to the physical. Normally, a unity of will and affection also arises between the mother and father. They both love their child, both want what's best for that child, both delight in the child's good fortune, and both mourn the child's misfortunes. Even in the case of divorce, very often the parents still share a united will to help their child and will put away their differences and become united again at important events in the child's life, like graduations and weddings.

Ideally, the unity of the parents includes running a household and raising the child together. They work together, as mother and father, to provide for the child's many needs. Their unity, which began as a unified sexual act, continues over the years as a unity of shared activity ordered to the education and raising of the child.

Children therefore help parents realize the goals of erotic love—to be together, unified physically, psychologically, socially, and emotionally. Each child unifies these two people together, and no one else, in a unity that is lasting and exclusive. Children are a good of marriage that unites the husband and wife in a way that realizes the aspirations of erotic love.

The use of contraception acts against the unity sought by erotic love. A couple only uses contraception when they do not want a child to unite them. Although their bodies are partially unified, the point of contraception is to make sure that there is *not* a complete unity between the two. Contraception, through various means, seeks to make sure that part of him (his sperm) does not unite with part of her (her egg). Contraception also denies, against the goals of erotic love, the acceptance of the whole person. Part of the person, the potential to become a father or a mother, the fertility of one or both parties, is intentionally rejected, at least for the time being. If this analysis is correct, then contraception does not serve the same goals as erotic love.

Does Having Children Foster Marital Friendship?

In marriage, husband and wife are not only erotic lovers but they can also share in the joys of friendship. Some people think that having children is the death of marriage. I'm going to suggest that just the opposite is true. Having children strengthens a marital friendship.

Aristotle believed that we could not be truly happy without friends, and I think he was right. Friendship involves mutual good will, common activity, and a shared emotional life. Each element is important for having a real friendship. We cannot be friends with someone who is not friends back. Friendly as we might be to them, real friendship is a two-way street requiring reciprocation. Similarly, friends don't just have good will for one another as fellow travelers might wish each other well. True friendship involves some sort of shared activity, be it mountain biking, analyzing fashion trends, or watching Monday Night Football. Finally, a real friend is someone who cares and shares in your triumphs and tragedies. They are happy with you; they are sad with you; and they accompany you on the up-and-down journey of life.

In marriage, husband and wife ideally enjoy not just erotic love, but also the joys of friendship. Having children, I'm going to suggest, strengthens this friendship.

Friendship first of all involves mutual good will, and having children reinforces that good will. Every marriage has its ups and downs, trials and tribulations. It is easy to become upset with a spouse and think, "I'm out of here. That's it. I give up." When there are children involved, a new consideration is in the mix. Leaving a spouse is not just leaving a spouse; it is also leaving the children or depriving the children of their father or mother. The love and affection parents have for their children also goes through its ups and downs, but—especially when the children are young—the natural protecting and nurturing instinct is strong. So, when children are in a marriage, the husband and the wife have an extra incentive to work things out, to forgive each other, and to reconcile, despite their disagreements and differences.

Similarly, children give rise to shared activity for the husband and wife. They share together in that singularly important project of procreating and educating their children. As a father myself, I know the frenzied shared activity of a household. Wake the kids up; get them in school clothes; make breakfast; attend to brushing teeth and asthma medication; drive to school; pick up from school, dancing lessons, and football practice; make dinner; oversee homework; say night prayers; and put them to bed. The typical problem for married couples with children is, not finding shared activity, but an excess of shared activity.

Finally, Aristotle pointed out that friends share in an emotional life together, but this too is greatly augmented by a husband and wife having children. Many moments in the child's life bring great, shared joy to the couple: birth, baptism, First Holy Communion, making varsity, graduating with honors. Many moments in the child's life bring shared distress to the couple: emergency-room visits, getting bullied or being the bully, failing the test, disobedience, the first failed romance. Whatever ups and downs come in the child's life, and there are many of both, the husband and wife share them together. They laugh, cry, worry, rejoice, and groan in union over the achievements and antics of their children.

Aristotle thought that the very best kinds of friends were "friends of virtue". Such friends are loved not for what they give us or for how they make us feel, but rather because they are a certain kind of person. Virtues are good habits built through repeated good actions. These stable dispositions make possible a self-mastery, ease, and joy in doing what is good and right. Hence, Aristotle reasons that a friendship of virtue will tend to be longer lasting than a friendship based on utility or pleasure.

Saint Thomas Aquinas wrote: "The greater a friendship is the more solid and long lasting will it be. Now there seems to be the greatest friendship between husband and wife, for they are united not only in the act of fleshly union, which produces a certain gentle association even among beasts, but also in the partnership of the whole range of domestic activity." [1] Husbands and

---

[1] Thomas Aquinas, *Summa contra Gentiles*, III:123:6.

wives can be friends of virtue, and having children greatly contributes to this kind of friendship.

To develop a virtue, a person needs to perform a good action over and over again. When a couple raises children together, they have abundant opportunities to develop these good habits. All the basic activities of childrearing— providing food, teaching children, transporting them back and forth, helping with homework—are good actions repeated over and over again, which develop virtues of generosity, self-sacrifice, patience, and responsibility in those who practice them. The more virtuous the husband and wife become, the stronger grows their friendship of virtue.

If anything indicates a failed marital friendship, it is divorce. Empirical evidence shows that having children lessens the likelihood of divorce.[2] Having children does not, of course, guarantee that a couple will not divorce, but it does lessen the likelihood of divorce.

Time and shared activity strengthen a friendship, and thus a marital friendship of virtue would have the conditions needed for the best kind of friendship. Particularly, the procreation and education of children can become a great bond between husband and wife. The generation of children is a shared, pleasurable activity that parents can share uniquely between them. Every child is a unique testimony to the union and activity existing between one man and one woman. A child is also the source of shared activity lasting a lifetime.

[2] David Bess, *The Evolution of Desire*, 4th edition (New York: Basic Books, 2003), p. 175.

Do Children Help Parents Get to Heaven?

I've gotten some great responses to the question, "What do children give to parents?" "Gray hair." "Ulcers." "Empty bank accounts." "No respect." There is more than an element of truth in these responses. It may have been an obvious advantage in ancient times to have many children to work in the fields, but how many people today agree with Saint Augustine that children are one of the blessings of marriage?

As a father, I've certainly had ups and downs with my children, including some major setbacks. But I'd like to propose that children actually help parents receive the most important good of all—eternal happiness. The *Baltimore Catechism* asks, "Why did God make you?" The answer reads, "God made me to know Him, to love Him, and to serve Him in this world, and to be happy with Him forever in heaven." As the late French poet Charles Péguy wrote, "In the end, life offers only one tragedy: not to have been a saint." [3] In other words, there is only one ultimate tragedy in life—not to go to heaven.

One man told me that he knew why children help their parents get to heaven: "You've got to go through hell to get to heaven." Jesus provided more reliable advice, "If you would enter life, keep the commandments" (Mt 19:17). Children help parents keep the commandments in a variety of ways.

For example, the fourth commandment is "Honor your father and mother." As teenagers and childless adults, it is

[3] As cited by Peter Kreeft, *Before I Go: Letters to Our Children about What Really Matters* (Lanham, Md.: Sheed & Ward, 2007), p. 23.

easy to slip into a hypercritical mode about our parents. They didn't provide enough of this, they gave way too much of that, they should have been different in so many ways. The imperfections of parents—even the best of parents—can be found by anyone who wants to find them.

Once someone begins to raise a child, however, the realization quickly dawns that parenthood is a tricky and difficult business. Competing responsibilities—work, household, financial, social—devour limited resources of time, energy, and attention. Before the first month is over, it becomes clear, all too clear, that despite the best of intentions, it is impossible to be a perfect parent with perfect children. As time goes on, particularly if there are multiple children, this realization is powerfully reinforced. But these failures and the inevitable stresses of parenthood allow us to reconsider our hasty judgments of our own parents. My mom and dad were not perfect, but neither am I a perfect parent. Indeed, in raising children ourselves, we come to realize just how difficult the parental task is, and just how much we owe our own parents for doing all the good things they did for us—minimally, keeping us alive, which is no small feat. Having kids makes it easier to keep the fourth commandment, "Honor your father and mother."

Raising children also helps a person keep the very first commandment, "I am the Lord your God. You shall have no gods before me." As children, we know we are not God. Someone else tells us when to go to bed, when to eat, when to work, and when to brush our teeth. We know we are not in charge of our own lives, let alone the universe.

As childless adults, it can be easier to forget that we are not God. We work where we want, do what we want, sleep, eat, and live as we want. We can come to feel, and sometimes even think, that we are in complete charge. The U.S. Supreme Court in its *Casey v. Planned Parenthood* decision reflects this view, "At the heart of liberty is the right to define one's own concept of existence, of meaning, of the universe, and of the mystery of human life." Each one of us is his own little god. The dimestore existentialism of the *Casey* decision echoes the atheistic philosopher Jean-Paul's Sartre's dictum that to be human is the desire to be God.

Sartre's desire to be God is thwarted by having children. We cannot choose whether they are shy or outgoing, athletic or clumsy, intelligent or slow. We get what we get. Even parents who adopt cannot comprehensively know who they are adopting, let alone parents who have biological children. Parents are also vulnerable in their children. The trials and tribulations of childhood and the teen years cannot always be fixed by mom and dad. When they suffer, we too suffer and realize our limitations. Most obviously, we cannot make our children always behave as we'd like. As babies, they cry out during church. As small children, they break and lose things. As teens, they rebel and test the boundaries of our patience. Mothers and fathers raising children realize, dramatically, repeatedly, and insistently, that they are not in charge, that they are not God. Such repeated realizations remove one obstacle to recognizing and worshipping the real God.

Having children also helps us to follow the teachings of Jesus. On the night before he died, Jesus told his disciples at the Last Supper, "This is my commandment, that you love one another as I have loved you" (Jn 15:12). God accepts us just as we are—with our sins, vices, and imperfections—but he loves us too much to allow us to remain just as we are, for he wants us to find true happiness in loving him and other people. In having children, good parents imitate God who loves each of us with *accepting love* and *transforming love*. William F. May notes, "Parents find it difficult to maintain an equilibrium between the two sides of love. . . . Accepting love, without transforming love, slides into indulgence and finally neglect. Transforming love, without accepting love, badgers and finally rejects." [4] Parents, in learning to love the way God loves, fulfill the commandment of Jesus.

One of the most disturbing and challenging passages in the Gospels talks about the Last Judgment, in which Christ the King will invite some people to heavenly glory, but condemn other people to exclusion forever from perfect happiness.

> Then the King will say to those at his right hand, "Come, O blessed of my Father, inherit the kingdom prepared for you from the foundation of the world; for I was hungry and you gave me food, I was thirsty and you gave me drink, I was a stranger and you welcomed me, I was naked and you clothed me, I was sick and you visited me, I was in prison and you came to me" (Mt 25:34–36).

Most people are not Missionaries of Charity like Mother Teresa. We do not do these kinds of things.

---

[4] William F. May as cited by Patrick Deneen, *Democratic Faith* (Princeton: Princeton University Press, 2005), p. 293.

Or do we? Every parent literally fulfills the tasks listed by Jesus. When children are hungry, we give them something to eat. When children are thirsty, we give them something to drink. All children come into the world as strangers, and we invite them into their homes. Children need clothes, and we clothe them. When children become sick, we look after them. When they are in trouble, we visit and help them. Perhaps on Judgment Day, parents—along with Mother Teresa—will enjoy hearing the words of Jesus, "[A]s you did it to one of the least of these my brethren, you did it to me" (Mt 25:40). Perhaps children—precisely in vulnerability and neediness—help their parents get to heaven.

Procreation, Contraception, and NFP

Procreation realizes the aims of erotic love, enhances the marital friendship of spouses, and helps parents get to heaven. Having children was fittingly described by Augustine, along with fidelity and the sacrament, as one of the goods of marriage. The Second Vatican Council taught: "Children are the supreme gift of marriage and contribute greatly to their parents flourishing" (*Gaudium et Spes*, no. 50). Procreation is a good, not just for those who come into existence, but also for their parents and others.

If we accept that procreation is a basic human good, what difference does that make for our understanding of contraception? Contraception—by definition—is an action against procreation. Pope Paul VI defined contraception as "any action which, whether in anticipation of a conjugal act, or in its accomplishment, or in the development of its natural consequences, whether as an end or as a means, is intended to prevent procreation" (*Humanae Vitae*, no. 14). Just as theft acts against the good of private property, just as lying acts against the good of truth, so too contraception acts against the good of the procreation of children.

But, someone might respond, surely parents should not have as many children as biologically possible? How can any couple shoulder the responsibility for seven, eight, nine, or even more children?

The Catholic Church does not teach that couples must have as many children as biologically possible. There is no rule about how many children a couple ought to have, and it is certainly *not* the case that all couples must have as many children as they are physically capable of bearing. Pope John Paul II spoke of "responsible parenthood", and by that he meant that the husband and wife should together determine their family size. It is their responsibility to do so—not the government's, not their pastor's, not their neighbor's responsibility. They should with wisdom and generosity seek out God's will for them in terms of having children. A couple might, in a given situation, come to the decision that they should not have another baby due to a variety of reasons.

In such situations, it is not the case that parents have only two choices—either have more children than they think they should have or use contraception. In some situations, a couple may decide that they ought not to have a child. I understand. When I was in graduate school at the University of Notre Dame, my yearly stipend was $10,000. Our apartment was so small that it could be vacuumed entirely from one outlet. We did not have health insurance, and we already had three children, the oldest of whom was three and a half years of age. My wife and I decided that this would not be a good time to have a fourth child, but we also knew that contraception was not the only alternative. So, we used natural family planning (NFP), sometimes also called fertility awareness-based methods (FAB methods), in order to delay having a baby.

What happened? It worked. There's an old joke, "What do you call people who use the rhythm method to avoid pregnancy?" "Parents." The rhythm method uses the *previous* cycle of the woman to determine when she is likely to be fertile in her *current* cycle. The rhythm method is, indeed, not reliable, since various factors such as stress and illness may alter the typical cycle of fertility in a given month. By contrast, NFP or FAB methods, unlike the rhythm method, chart signs of fertility in the *current* cycle. Are such methods effective? According to a variety of studies, NFP, or FAB, is similar in effectiveness to the contraceptive pill. "Researchers have found that a method of natural family planning that uses two indicators to identify the fertile phase in a woman's menstrual cycle is as effective as the contraceptive pill for avoiding unplanned pregnancies if used correctly, according to a report published online in Europe's leading reproductive medicine journal *Human Reproduction*."[5] Unlike the contraceptive pill, FAB has no harmful chemical side

[5] See "Natural Family Planning Method as Effective as Contraceptive Pill, New Research Finds", *Science Daily*, February 21, 2007, http://www.sciencedaily.com/releases/2007/02/070221065200.htm (accessed November 19, 2010).

effects, is inexpensive, and engages both the man and the woman in reproductive decisions.

The well-documented effectiveness of NFP raises another question: What then is the difference between FAB and contraception? If NFP and the pill, when used properly, are equally effective in preventing pregnancy, what then is the difference? Isn't NFP just another form of contraception?

It is true that users of contraception and users of NFP/FAB may have the same *motivation* when they choose these methods, namely, to delay pregnancy. It is also true that users of NFP/FAB and contraception may be in the same *circumstances*, circumstances that prompt them, as responsible parents, to decide that right now is not a good time to achieve a pregnancy. But when analyzing the ethics of any action, it is important to take into consideration, not just the circumstances and not just the motivation, but also the action itself or the means chosen to realize the motivation. Just as a good airline pilot must have good vision, experience flying, and sobriety (and two of these three is not enough), so too for an action as a whole to be a good action, all the elements of the action must be good—circumstances, motivation, and the act itself.

So, is the act of using NFP/FAB simply another form of contraception? As noted, contraception is defined as any action taken either before, during, or after sexual intercourse which is specifically intended to render the sexual act nonprocreative. If contraception acts against the human good of procreation, and acting against a human good is morally wrong, then it follows that contraception is wrong. Users of NFP/FAB methods are not using contraception, since they do nothing to render their sexual acts nonprocreative. Rather, if they chose to delay pregnancy, they are choosing not to have sexual intercourse. They cannot at the same time also choose to render their sexual acts infertile, since there are no sexual acts rendered infertile. If they choose to have sex later, during a time of infertility, likewise they are not doing anything before, during, or after sexual intercourse to render their sexual acts nonprocreative. So NFP is not a form of contraception.

Of course, the typical results or consequences of contraception and NFP are similar—no pregnancy is achieved. But it does not follow from this that FAB and contraception are morally equivalent. It is also true that those who lie and those who simply do not say anything similarly leave people unaware of the truth, but there is an important moral difference, other things being equal, between lying about something and simply not saying something. Every day, each one of us omits to tell others all sorts of things, perhaps what we had for breakfast or how much money we made last year, but this does not mean that every day each one of us lies. We can only lie if we choose to communicate about something *and* we communicate what we believe to be false. If we choose not to communicate about some matter, then we cannot at the same time also choose to lie about that matter. Similarly, if we choose not to have sex, we cannot at the same time choose to use contraception, since contraception is by definition about rendering sexual acts infertile.

Blessed John Henry Cardinal Newman, the great Oxford convert to Catholicism, wrote a beautiful sermon about a venture of faith. In it, he asked, if you found out that Christianity was false, demonstrably false, would your life change? If your life would be exactly the same, even if they found the bones of Jesus in the grave and so Christianity was false, then you have not yet made a venture of faith. Most of us, I certainly count myself among them, have not ventured terribly much in faith. We are not missionaries in foreign lands; we have not given up husband or wife, children, or property for the sake of the Kingdom. But one venture we can make is to live, as best as we can, according to the teachings of Christ's Church even in areas where these teachings challenge us. The most difficult teachings have nothing to do directly with contraception: forgive those who wrong you; love those who hate you; do good to your enemies. We all are called to give ourselves totally to the service of God, even when it means following difficult teachings such as contraception.

The Fifth Big Myth

The Church Hates Gays:
The Myth of Catholic "Homophobia" and Inaction against AIDS/HIV

Few topics are more painful or delicate in the contemporary world than the Catholic Church and homosexuality. Perhaps only on a par with a discussion of abortion, the issues raised by homosexuality stir up bitter emotions and intense disagreements. Much of this intense contention is based on misunderstandings about what the Church does and does not teach about the issues of homosexuality.

Many people seem to think that the Catholic Church teaches that, "God hates fags." For this reason, they also believe the Catholic Church opposes the distribution of condoms because the Church considers the life of gay men to be unimportant and not valuable enough to protect.

These statements are false. The Catholic Church could not disagree more with such statements of bigotry as "God hates fags." The Church teaches, "It is deplorable that homosexual persons have been and are the object of violent malice in speech or in action. Such treatment deserves condemnation from the Church's pastors wherever it occurs."[1] God loves everyone, regardless of sexual orientation, regardless of anything, and this is a basis for the intrinsic dignity of every single person. God's love includes every single man on earth unconditionally—gay, straight, bisexual, or whatever the case may be. Unfortunately, it is true that some Catholics fail to accept and live out the Church's teaching on this matter, as in so many other matters as well. However, the message of Jesus, the message echoed by the Church, is that everyone person should love, value, and respect every other person, without exception and without condition.

God's love for us expresses itself through his creating us and calling us to be happy, truly happy. The teachings of Jesus are meant for everyone; the suffering, death, and Resurrection of Jesus are meant for everyone; the salvation won by Jesus is offered to everyone. Those who believe in God, the God of love, have an obligation to discern God's will and try to live it out. For whatever the God of love asks us to do, he only asks for our own well-being and the well-being of others. For Christians, God's love is known especially through the work and message of Jesus. Jesus did not explicitly address the issue of homosexual acts, but Jesus did emphasize the importance of marriage between a man and a woman (Jn 2:1–11) and confirmed the sinfulness of sexual activity outside of marriage (Jn 8:1–11; Jn 4:16–18). It is not surprising that Jesus did not say much about these matters, since his view was typical of the Jewish community of his time,

---

[1] Congregation for the Doctrine of the Faith (CDF), "Letter to the Bishops of the Catholic Church on the Pastoral Care of Homosexual People" (1986), no. 10.

who agreed on the importance of limiting sexual activity to within marriage and viewed fertility as a great blessing. Similarly, Jesus did not emphasize that there is only *one* God or that one should not kill newborn babies, since his Jewish interlocutors had long ago rejected the pagan practices of polytheism and infanticide. Jesus gave his apostles authority to teach in his name, to point the way to true happiness by doing the will of the Father in heaven.

In the previous chapter, we addressed the importance of all sexual acts being open to life. Because sexual activity between two men or between two women cannot be open to life, such activity is incompatible with the proper ordering of sexual activity. In the next chapter, we will address the importance of marriage and the nature of marriage as a comprehensive union of a man and a woman. If a same-sex couple cannot be married, this adds another dimension to the consideration of homosexual activity. If all sexual activity should be confined to marriage, and marriage is impossible between two people of the same sex, then people of the same sex should not engage in sexual activity.

One common misconception that many people share is that the Catholic Church has some special animus against homosexuals. For most of history, not just the Church but society in general did not have a category of "homosexual" or "bisexual" people as opposed to "heterosexual" people. Similarly, today, we do not have a specific category or identity for, say, men who love slender women of Nordic descent. Even though there are such men, they do not self-identify nor are they identified by others as a particular "kind" of person based on this characteristic.

In a similar way, prior to the nineteenth century, people were not identified as nor did they understand themselves to be "gay", "lesbian", or "straight", as is today common. They may have engaged in homosexual activity, but that did not make them a specific kind of person any more than having sex with a tall person with green eyes makes someone have a particular kind of (sexual) identity.

The Church's teaching focuses not on the *identities* of certain kinds of people, but on the *actions* chosen by anyone. The previous chapter explored the Catholic view that life and love, procreative possibility and sexual union, should not be disunited. In terms of sexual activity, the actions chosen by people ought to be open to life and within marriage. This is true for a man and woman within marriage as well as for everyone else. There is a single standard for everyone.

Many people assume that unless a person is regularly engaging in sexual activity, then the person will not be happy or fulfilled in life. This assumption is challenged by Sherif Girgis, Robert P. George, and Ryan T. Anderson, who write that it is a mistaken assumption that sexual activity is necessary for a fulfilled life:

> [This idea] devalues many people's way of life. What we wish for people unable to marry because of a lack of any attraction to a member of the opposite sex is the same as what we wish for people who cannot marry for any other reason: rich and fulfilling lives. In the splendor of human variety, these can take infinitely many forms. In any of them, energy that would otherwise go into marriage is channeled toward ennobling endeavors: deeper devotion to

family or nation, service, adventure, art, or a thousand other things.[2]

The difficulty of living the Church's teachings on sexuality impinges on virtually everyone to a greater or lesser degree; it does not single out people with same-sex attraction. As Girgis, George, and Anderson note,

> people ... suppose that traditional morality unfairly singles out people who experience same-sex attractions. Far from it. In everyone, traditional morality sees foremost a person of dignity whose welfare makes demands on every other being that can hear and answer them. In everyone, it sees some desires that cannot be integrated with the comprehensive union of marriage. In everyone, it sees the radical freedom to make choices that transcend those inclinations, heredity, and hormones; enabling men and women to become authors of their own character.[3]

To become a person of good character requires effort and struggle, regardless of the kind of struggle involved. Married couples struggle not to use contraception and to be faithful to their vows of fidelity; single people struggle to wait until marriage; people who have taken vows of celibacy struggle to live their commitment; persons with homosexual inclinations struggle not to engage in homosexual behavior.

The struggle of the homosexual person who wants to live according to the Church's teaching can be particularly difficult. But the difficulty of the Church's teaching on sexual matters, including homosexuality, is no

[2] Sherif Girgis, Robert P. George, and Ryan T. Anderson, "What Is Marriage?" *Harvard Journal of Law & Public Policy* 43, no. 1 (2010): 245–87, at 282.
[3] Ibid., p. 284.

greater—indeed it is less—than the difficulty of many of her other teachings. How many Christian people can honestly say that they have not failed to follow the teachings of Jesus? Do we love God with our whole heart, soul, mind, and strength? Do we love our neighbor as ourselves? Do we forgive and pray for our enemies? Unfortunately, many people believe—falsely—that sexual sins are the very worst kinds of sins, but at least according to Saint Thomas Aquinas, this is not the case. The greatest virtue is charity, not chastity, and to sin against the love of God is much more serious than to sin through weakness in a sexual way. In the Catholic view, people regularly separate themselves from the love of God and neighbor, and this separation is known as sin. Everyone is therefore in need of God's great mercy, and the only kinds of people excluded from God's mercy are the ones who exclude themselves.

One of the main flash points of criticism against the Catholic Church is her position on the use of condoms to combat HIV/AIDS. For example, Richard Dawkins writes that the Catholic Church sends "its missionaries out to tell deliberate lies to AIDS-weakened Africans, about the alleged ineffectiveness of condoms in protecting against HIV".[4] Edward C. Green, director of the AIDS Prevention Research at Harvard University, disagrees. When asked, "Is Pope Benedict being criticized unfairly for his comments about HIV and condoms?" Green

[4] Richard Dawkins, "On Faith Panelists Blog: Give Us Your Misogynists and Bigots", http://onfaith.washingtonpost.com/onfaith/panelists/richard_dawkins/2009/10/give_us_your_misogynists_and_bigots.html (accessed January 12, 2012).

responded, "This is hard for a liberal like me to admit, but yes, it's unfair because in fact, the best evidence we have supports his comments." [5] Dr. Green's credentials as an expert in the field of HIV/AIDS prevention include serving on the United States Presidential Advisory Council on HIV/AIDS and on the AIDS Research Advisory Council for the National Institutes of Health. Green's survey of the published scientific studies treating this question indicate that the pope's view is correct:

In 2003, Norman Hearst and Sanny Chen of the University of California conducted a condom effectiveness study for the United Nations' AIDS program and found no evidence of condoms working as a primary HIV-prevention measure in Africa. UNAIDS quietly disowned the study. (The authors eventually managed to publish their findings in the quarterly *Studies in Family Planning.*) Since then, major articles in other peer-reviewed journals such as the *Lancet*, *Science* and *BMJ* [*British Medical Journal*] have confirmed that condoms have not worked as a primary intervention in the population-wide epidemics of Africa. In a 2008 article in *Science* called "Reassessing HIV Prevention" 10 AIDS experts concluded that "consistent condom use has not reached a sufficiently high level, even after many years of widespread and often aggressive promotion, to produce a measurable slowing of new infections in the generalized epidemics of Sub-Saharan Africa." [6]

[5] Timothy Morgan, "Condoms, HIV, and Pope Benedict: Leading HIV Researcher Edward C. Green Says Criticism of the Pope 'Unfair'", *Christianity Today*, March 20, 2009, http://www.christianitytoday.com/ct/2009/marchweb-only/111-53.0.html (accessed March 6, 2012).

[6] Edward Green, "Condoms, HIV-AIDS and Africa—The Pope Was Right", *The Washington Post*, Sunday, March 29, 2009, http://www.washingtonpost.com/wp-dyn/content/article/2009/03/27/AR2009032702825.html (accessed October 19, 2010).

In Green's view, different strategies of AIDS/HIV infection are appropriate for different cultural situations. For the record, Green does not oppose the use of condoms to reduce the risk of HIV, but he also rejects exporting a "one-size-fits-all" Western solution of condom distribution throughout the world.

Why has condom distribution not effectively reduced African AIDS? Green writes, "One reason is 'risk compensation.' That is, when people think they're made safe by using condoms at least some of the time, they actually engage in riskier sex." [7] In other words, widespread condom use may lull some people into engaging in risky behaviors that they otherwise would not have chosen because such behaviors are now viewed as safe. Green notes a study in the *Journal of Acquired Immune Deficiency Syndrome* which "followed two groups of young people in Uganda, and the group that had the intensive condom promotion actually were found to have a greater number of sex partners. So that cancels out the risk reduction that the technology of condoms ought to provide." [8] Risk compensation or behavioral disinhibition prompted by condom use may overall increase the likelihood of contracting HIV by increasing the number of partners chosen and the frequency of risky behavior. Any given sex act may be less risky with a condom than without a condom, but the use, promotion, and availability of condoms may lead to many people choosing

[7] Ibid.

[8] P. Kajubi, et al., "Increasing Condom Use without Reducing HIV Risk: Results of a Controlled Community Trial in Uganda", *Journal of Acquired Immune Deficiency Syndrome* 40 (2005): 77–82.

to engage in risky behavior who otherwise would not have chosen this behavior. This factor, risk compensation or behavioral disinhibition, applies to the promotion and availability of condoms not just in Africa but also elsewhere.

Other aspects of the AIDS problem in Africa reflect widespread sexual practices that are less widespread outside Africa.

> Another factor is that people seldom use condoms in steady relationships because doing so would imply a lack of trust, [writes Green]. However, it's those ongoing relationships that drive Africa's worst epidemics. In these, most HIV infections are found in general populations, not in high-risk groups such as sex workers, gay men or persons who inject drugs. And in significant proportions of African populations, people have two or more regular sex partners who overlap in time. In Botswana, which has one of the world's highest HIV rates, 43 percent of men and 17 percent of women surveyed had two or more regular sex partners in the previous year. These ongoing multiple concurrent sex partnerships resemble a giant, invisible web of relationships through which HIV/AIDS spreads. A study in Malawi showed that even though the average number of sexual partners was only slightly over two, fully two-thirds of this population was interconnected through such networks of overlapping, ongoing relationships.[9]

These overlapping relationships fuel the spread of HIV in Africa.

So, how should we try to combat HIV/AIDS in Africa? Green believes that the best strategy is not an emphasis

---

[9] Green, "Condoms, HIV-AIDS and Africa".

on condoms but rather an emphasis on fidelity. "In Uganda's early, largely home-grown AIDS program, which began in 1986, the focus was on 'Sticking to One Partner' or 'Zero Grazing' (which meant remaining faithful within a polygamous marriage) and 'Loving Faithfully.' These simple messages worked."[10] The Catholic emphasis on fidelity within marriage and monogamy reinforces these simple but effective messages for preventing HIV/AIDS.

Green summarized his book *Rethinking AIDS Prevention* as follows:

> The largely medical solutions funded by major donors have had little impact in Africa, the continent hardest hit by AIDS. Instead, relatively simple, low-cost behavioral change programs—stressing increased monogamy and delayed sexual activity for young people—have made the greatest headway in fighting or preventing the disease's spread. Ugandans pioneered these simple, sustainable interventions and achieved significant results.[11]

Though these conclusions fly in the face of ideological commitments to fighting HIV/AIDS by condoms, condoms, and condoms, Green's book received a review in the *Journal of the American Medical Association*. "If Green's analysis is correct, we are faced with a troubling paradox: while our technologically sophisticated system often operates at the margin of acceptable cost efficacy, halfway around the world, secular bias and biomedical fiscal

---

[10] Ibid.
[11] See http://en.wikipedia.org/wiki/Edward_C._Green (accessed July 25, 2011).

power are responsible for discouraging and discrediting simple yet effective solutions, at the cost of millions of lives." [12] It turns out then that pushing condoms costs lives, but the message of Pope Benedict and the Catholic Church—abstinence prior to marriage and fidelity within marriage—served to save lives.

Pope Benedict's views began the topic of worldwide conversation again at the release of his book-length interview with journalist Peter Seewald, called *The Light of the World*. In this book, Pope Benedict said:

> There may be a basis in the case of some individuals, as perhaps when a male prostitute uses a condom, where this can be a first step in the direction of a moralization, a first assumption of responsibility, on the way toward recovering an awareness that not everything is allowed and that one cannot do whatever one wants. But it is not really the way to deal with the evil of HIV infection. That can really lie only in a humanization of sexuality. [13]

This quotation was interpreted by some as giving a "green light" for the use of condoms.

This impression is dispelled, however, by the pope's answer to Seewald's next question, "Are you saying, then, that the Catholic Church is actually not opposed in principle to the use of condoms?" Benedict answered: "She of course does *not* regard it as a real or moral solution, but, in this or that case, there can be nonetheless, in the intention of reducing the risk of infection, a first step in

[12] *Journal of the American Medical Association* 293, no. 17 (2005): 2162.

[13] Pope Benedict XVI, *Light of the World* (San Francisco: Ignatius Press, 2010), p. 119.

a movement toward a different way, a more human way, of living sexuality." [14]

Pope Benedict is not in this exchange adopting the view that the use of condoms is morally acceptable, though widely broadcasted media distortions gave that impression. Rather, he is drawing on a long tradition in ethics that draws an important distinction between the *act itself* and the *motivation* with which an action is performed. It is not that the act itself of using a condom during sex is morally acceptable, which is why Benedict says that the use of condoms is not "a real or moral solution". Rather, Pope Benedict is saying that the intention which motivates using a condom in such a situation (i.e., the intention not to harm others by spreading disease) is laudable, and, one hopes, a first step toward understanding the true purposes of sexual activity—which for him would include the reaffirmation of the love and commitment of husband and wife as well as an openness to procreation.

The Church's response to HIV/AIDS is not just a matter of words, the pope's or anyone else's, but primarily of deeds. The U.S. Catholic bishops, for example, have done a great deal in the fight against HIV/AIDS through the following means in their dioceses:

- providing education on HIV/AIDS at the parish and diocesan school levels;

- providing basic health services and spiritual support to people living with HIV/AIDS;

[14] Ibid., emphasis added.

- directing members of our parishes to places where they can be tested for HIV infection;

- planning a faith conference, town-hall meeting, or workshop about the impact of HIV/AIDS on our parishes and communities;

- planning a prayer vigil to remember those who have died from AIDS and for those still fighting HIV/AIDS;

- organizing parish ministry visits to people with HIV/AIDS in hospitals, in nursing homes, or at their homes;

- organizing a parish or community event for annual national HIV/AIDS observances such as World AIDS Day on December 1 or National HIV Testing Day on June 27;

- educating to fight stigma and discrimination against persons living with HIV/AIDS.[15]

This support of those suffering was begun at the very beginning of the AIDS crisis when the Archbishop of New York, John Cardinal O'Connor, founded New York City's first hospital unit dedicated to caring for AIDS patients. In unannounced visits in the night, Cardinal O'Connor would care for gay men dying of the disease, changing their bedpans and cleaning their sores. Likewise, Mother Teresa and her Missionaries of Charity cared for thousands and thousands of people suffering from

---

[15] See "Hispanic/Latino Affairs", http://www.usccb.org/hispanicaffairs/hivaids.shtml (accessed December 2, 2010).

HIV/AIDS. The practical work of Cardinal O'Connor and Mother Teresa caring for those suffering from AIDS continues today throughout the entire world. "Across its global works the Catholic church provides roughly a quarter of the medical care for the over 33 million people worldwide afflicted with HIV/AIDS—including close to half the total treatment efforts in Africa, where two-thirds of the stricken live." [16] The Church shows her love for people suffering from AIDS, daily, effectively, and unreservedly. Such service is an expression of love, a love for all people.

[16] Rocco Palmo, "The Many Faces of AIDS", http://whispersintheloggia. blogspot.com/2010/12/on-world-day-many-faces-of-aids.html (accessed December 1, 2010).

The Sixth Big Myth

The Church Opposes Same-Sex Marriage Because of Bigotry: The Myth That There Is No Rational Basis for Limiting Marriage to One Man and One Woman

People often hold that the Catholic Church's opposition to same-sex marriage is unreasonable, bigoted, and irrational. So as to have a full debate about this important issue, rather than simply calling names and engaging in *ad hominem* attacks against either side, three major questions should be considered. First, is a ban on same-sex marriage like a ban on interracial marriage? Secondly, what are the arguments in favor of same-sex marriage (SSM)? And finally, if SSM were legalized, would it really harm anyone or anything, including traditional marriage? Although much has been written about each of these questions, at this stage of the debate it is possible to give an overview of each of the major answers to each of these questions.

San Francisco Judge Vaughn Walker, who overturned Proposition 8 (which reads in its entirety: "Only marriage between a man and a woman is valid or recognized in California"), writes, "Proposition 8 singles out gays and lesbians and legitimates their unequal treatment. Proposition 8 perpetuates the stereotype that gays and lesbians are incapable of forming long-term loving relationships and that gays and lesbians are not good parents." [1] But the proposition says nothing at all about gays or lesbians, nor does it assume that gays and lesbians are incapable of forming long-term, loving relationships or of being good parents. A majority of Californians, indeed a majority of Americans, as well as President Barack Obama (before his position revolved for the third time), oppose same-sex marriage, and it is unfair of Walker to attribute to such a diverse group the views ascribed. It is an *ad hominem* attack, not a civil engagement with opposing views, to allege that all opposition to same-sex marriage is rooted in hatred, fear, or condemnation of homosexuals.

Some people say that denial of same-sex marriage is like denial of marriage between the races. It was wrong to ban interracial marriage, so too it is wrong to ban same-sex marriage. Walker points to important Supreme Court precedents such as *Loving v. Virginia*, which allowed for interracial marriage and struck down antimiscegenation laws. But is banning interracial marriage really like banning same-sex marriage?

Interestingly, those who have the most bitter and deep experience of discrimination in our country, African-Americans, do not share this judgment. Some 70 percent

[1] Vaughn R. Walker, *Perry v. Schwarzenegger*, No. C-09-2292, United States Court of Appeals, Ninth Circuit, www.latimes.com/media/acrobat/2010-08/55367172.pdf.

of African-Americans voted in favor of Prop 8 in California, defining marriage as between one man and one woman. In fact, differences in race are not equivalent to differences in sex. Everyone agrees it is wrong to have "separate but equal" facilities for each race—for example, bathrooms for only African-Americans. But virtually everyone agrees it is fine to have separate women's bathrooms and men's bathrooms. We have separate men's and women's Olympic basketball teams, but we would not accept a white U.S. basketball team and an African-American U.S. basketball team. The analogy between banning interracial marriage and banning same-sex marriage fails because discrimination according to race is wrong, but distinctions ("separate but equal") according to sex is not *always* wrong.

Walker also writes, "Proposition 8 places the force of law behind stigmas against gays and lesbians, including: Gays and lesbians do not have intimate relationships similar to heterosexual couples; gays and lesbians are not as good as heterosexuals; and gay and lesbian relationships do not deserve the full recognition of society." [2] Again, the proposition says nothing of the kind.

His implicit argument seems to be that if two men or two women have an intimate relationship with each other, they should be allowed to get married. The implied premise is that whoever has love and commitment should be allowed to get married. Clearly, this premise is false. True love and commitment exist in many intimate relationships that should not be recognized as marriage. For example, a

---

[2] Ibid., p. 85.

grandson and a grandmother, or an army platoon, can have true love and commitment to each other, but they have no right to marry. These intimate relationships are not based on erotic love or sexual activity, but they are not necessarily less intimate or important on this account. So, the argument on the basis of love and commitment fails to establish that same-sex marriage is justified.

In truth, the traditional marriage law is neutral with respect to sexual orientation. The law does not say that gays and lesbians are not as good as heterosexuals; indeed, the law says nothing whatsoever about sexual orientation. Any unmarried man and unmarried woman can marry each other, regardless of the sexual orientation of either party. As the marriage law is neutral with respect to race and religion, so too it is neutral with respect to sexual orientation, treating all people equally.

Same-sex marriage advocates will object that even though homosexuals can and do currently get married, they cannot marry in accordance with their sexual orientation—for example, a gay man cannot marry a man. Same-sex marriage secures the right of people to marry in accordance with their sexual orientation.

However, if there is a right to marry in accordance with sexual orientation, then a bisexual should be allowed to marry both a man and a woman at the same time. Thus, bigamy would have to be acceptable. If a bisexual were forced to choose between marrying either a man or a woman, then the bisexual would not be allowed to marry in accordance with the bisexual orientation.

It could be objected that although the bisexual may be *attracted* to both males and females, he must choose in marriage just one person. In a similar way, a heterosexual male may be attracted to several females, but in marriage he must choose just one woman. This objection fails, however. If allowed only to marry one person, the bisexual would be forced to marry *as if* he had a homosexual orientation or *as if* he had a heterosexual orientation. Neither decision for a man or for a woman corresponds to his orientation, which is not to men alone or to women alone but to both men and women. In choosing just one partner, the bisexual would alienate himself from half of his orientation. By contrast, a heterosexual man marrying a woman does marry in accordance with his orientation, which is toward the female sex.

Of course, human sexual desire is not limited to heterosexuality, homosexuality, and bisexuality. If it were true that people had a right to marry in accordance with their sexual orientation, we would have to extend this right to other forms of sexuality. Zoosexuality (attraction to animals) justifies human-and-animal marriage (HAM). Necrosexuality (sexual attraction to corpses) justifies the dead–and–alive marriage (DAM). Autosexuality (sexual attraction to oneself) justifies self-marriage (SEM).

Someone might respond that these examples are absurd, that no one seeks these kinds of "marriages". Of course, the same thing would have been said just a few years ago about same-sex unions. In fact, people sometimes do seek these kinds of "marriages". As the *Shanghai Daily* reported, "Chen Wei-yih has posed for a set of photos in a flowing white dress, enlisted a wedding planner and rented a banquet hall for a marriage celebration with 30 friends. But there is no groom. Chen will marry herself." [3] An episode of Jerry Springer was titled, "I married a horse." Clearly, each sexual orientation does not justify a corresponding kind of marriage.

Of course, the advocate for SSM can reply that autosexuality, necrosexuality, and zoosexuality are very rare, unlike homosexuality or heterosexuality. But in protecting minority rights, the numbers of people in a given class are irrelevant. Why should the marriage rights of some sexual minorities (such as same-sex marriage) be protected but not the rights of other sexual minorities (SEM, HAM, DAM)?

Advocates of SSM may also object that many people believe that *free consent* is an *essential* part of marriage and that free consent can *only* be given by living humans, but not in HAM or DAM.

"Free consent" is indeed an essential part of marriage as traditionally defined. However, SSM by its nature challenges marriage as traditionally defined, so SSM cannot consistently appeal to the definition of traditional marriage. Also, free consent *can* be given for bigamy and self-marriage, so this reply does not fully respond to the critique of the premise that people have a right to marry in accordance with their sexual orientation.

Someone might object that free consent is essential for marriage, not because it is essential to the traditional definition, but rather because without free consent there is a violation of another's autonomy. However, the dead

---

[3] See http://www.shanghaidaily.com/article/list.asp?id=3&type=National (accessed October, 23, 2010).

and animals do not have autonomy, so there is no autonomy to be violated in these cases. The point is *not* that
same-sex marriage is the same thing as marriage between
a living person and a corpse or marriage between living
people and animals. A union between two people of
the same sex is a union of two people with intrinsic
dignity, inestimable value, and equal human rights—
which is not true of a corpse or an animal. The point
is rather that the arguments used to justify same-sex marriage would equally justify HAM or DAM, so these arguments are not a sound justification for SSM.

This equal dignity shared by all humans—including,
of course, all people regardless of their sexual orientation—is used as a basis for arguing for SSM. Since all
persons, gay or straight, have the same basic dignity, institutionalized forms of lesser regard for some persons are
wrong. But limiting marriage to heterosexual couples
disrespects homosexual persons. Therefore, reserving marriage for heterosexual couples is wrong.

The major premise is true: all people, regardless of sexual orientation or any other condition, have the same
basic dignity, and institutionalized forms of lesser regard
for some persons are wrong. But is the minor premise
true? We cannot hold that "reserving marriage for heterosexual couples" is "a way of institutionalizing the lesser
regard in which homosexual loves—and thereby homosexual persons are held", since we could just as well say:

- Reserving marriage for couples is a way of institutionalizing the lesser regard in which autosexual
  loves—and thereby autosexual persons—are held.

- Reserving marriage for couples is a way of institutionalizing the lesser regard in which polyamorous loves—and thereby polyamorous persons—are held.

- Reserving marriage for humans is a way of institutionalizing the lesser regard in which human-animal loves—and thereby persons who love animals—are held.

- Reserving marriage for living people is a way of institutionalizing the lesser regard in which living-deceased loves—and thereby persons who love the deceased—are held.

In other words, the minor premise is not true. I am not, lest I be misunderstood, saying that homosexual persons are equivalent to persons who have a sexual orientation toward themselves, animals, or corpses. What I am saying is that all people, regardless of whatever sexual orientation they have, be it common and widely accepted or extremely rare and socially maligned, have intrinsic dignity. However, it does not follow from the intrinsic dignity of each individual that there ought to be a socially recognized form of marriage corresponding to the desires of each individual person.

Perhaps the most common argument used by SSM advocates is the marriage-equality argument. It is wrong to oppose equal rights for everyone, including equal rights to marry whomever we love. Banning same-sex marriage opposes equal rights for everyone. Therefore, it is wrong to ban same-sex marriage.

The major premise, in the italicized portion, is false: "It is wrong to oppose equal rights for everyone, including *equal rights to marry whomever we love*." Some people love those who are already married to someone else, or those who do not want to marry them, or their close blood relatives, or prepubescent children, or animals, or nonliving things. Denial of SSM does not undermine the equality before the law of people who desire it, any more than denial of bigamy, polygamy, HAM, or DAM undermines the basic equality of the people who desire these kinds of unions to be declared marriages. To say that banning same-sex marriage opposes equal rights for everyone again proves too much, since we could just as well say: Banning polygamous marriage, self-marriage, human-animal marriage, or human–inanimate object marriage opposes equal rights for everyone. The principles invoked to justify same-sex marriage also justify kinds of "marriages" that virtually no one accepts, so these principles ought to be rejected.

The minor premise of the equality argument is also problematic: "Banning same-sex marriage opposes equal rights for everyone." What does "equal rights" really mean? Equality does not treat every person or every group in exactly the same way. Equality treats persons or groups that are the same in the same way but not persons or groups that are significantly different. For example, an air marshal can carry a gun on a plane, but regular citizens cannot. A sixteen-year-old can drive a car but a ten-year-old cannot. Such limitations are justly made despite rare exceptions (e.g., the unusual ten-year-old who is more mature than the average sixteen-year-old; the regular citizen who is better suited to defend the innocent passengers on the plane than the air marshal). The question is, are there any significant differences between same-sex couples and opposite-sex couples that justify treating them differently?

Thus far I've simply sought to undermine the arguments for same-sex marriage, but it is also important to try to establish the rational justification for limiting marriage to the union of a man and a woman. Opposite-sex couples can do what no other kind of union (same-sex, human-nonhuman, living-nonliving) can do.

Marriage, everyone agrees, involves a kind of union. But what kind of union? What makes marriage different from friendships, which also involve unions of various kinds? What activity makes marriage unique and different from the wide variety of human relationships?

What makes marriage different is that it is a *comprehensive* union.[4] A comprehensive union is one that unites the two people, not just in terms of finances (business partners could do that) or activities (tennis partners have that), but in the deepest way possible. To be united, persons have to unite in a spiritual way as well as in an organic, bodily way. Spiritually, a couple becomes united when they make and live out the vows of marriage, "I take you to be my wife/husband in good times and in bad, in sickness and in health, until death do us part. I will love you and honor you all the days of our life." Bodily, they become one in the act of sexual intercourse. Their bodily unity is, not just a rubbing against one

---

[4] Sherif Girgis, Robert P. George, and Ryan T. Anderson, "What Is Marriage?", *Harvard Journal of Law & Public Policy* 43, no. 1 (2010): 245–87, at 266–68.

another, but true unity in which the two become one in such a way that they can generate another one.

This organic physical unity is more profound than that which can take place in other sorts of sexual activity. Even adolescents understand that there is something unique about sexual intercourse (coitus), a more profound kind of unity than that which takes place in other kinds of sexual activity. When teenagers ask their friends, "Did you get to first base, second base, third base, or home plate?" they reflect a true understanding, however immaturely expressed, that not all kinds of sexual activity are equally profound, equally uniting of a couple. Only an opposite-sex couple can "go all the way" in terms of a comprehensive *bodily* union. Without "going all the way", a couple is simply not comprehensively united. Since marriage is a comprehensive unity, if a couple cannot "go all the way", then they cannot be married.

Only couples of the opposite sex can do acts that unite them in a bodily way, in an organic way, so only opposite-sex couples can achieve a comprehensive union of spirit and body. But if marriage is precisely a comprehensive union, then only opposite-sex couples can get married. Other kinds of relationships can achieve unity on a wide variety of levels, but only a man and a woman can achieve the deepest kind of unity, on not just a spiritual but also a bodily level.

Only a male and a female of a certain age can together engage in acts of a reproductive kind, acts that unite them in an organic, bodily way. Because of the significance of this activity, one essential to the survival of society, it is proper to recognize and socially promote the unique value of a relationship between a man and a woman of reproductive age. No same-sex couples, nor the other kinds of unions mentioned earlier, can become united in this way, so that their bodies function together in a uniquely significant activity. Because of an interest in future generations of citizens, the state has a significant interest in promoting opposite-sex couples rather than other kinds of couples.

This basis makes sense of the other limitations to marriage currently in place. A person does not have to be eighteen to be married (at least in the United States and also in most other countries). In many states and countries, females can marry at a younger age than males (e.g., in New Hampshire, females can marry at age thirteen, but males must be fourteen). The age limitations are obviously related to potential fertility, which begins before age eighteen and which begins earlier in females than males. Many of these age limitations do not even require parental consent (even for fourteen-year-olds) if the woman is pregnant or has given birth to the man's child, again pointing to the reproductive significance of marriage.

The link between marriage and reproduction also makes sense of other limitations on marriage. Virtually all U.S. states and other countries deny a right to marry close blood relatives. Here too, the reason is linked to fertility, since offspring of close blood relatives have a higher risk of genetic deformity. Many of these laws make exceptions for older couples (say, after sixty-five) when fertility is no longer in play. Thus, limiting marriage to couples of a (healthy) reproductive kind is not arbitrary or discriminatory or opposed to equality, any more than the other limitations already in the law.

Advocates of SSM object that not all married couples have children. As a society, we allow infertile, elderly women who can no longer have children to marry. Since we do not check whether an opposite-sex couple intends to have children or is able to have children, marriage in our society does not have an essential link to reproduction. And since marriage does not have an essential link to reproduction, same-sex couples should also be permitted to be married.

The reply to this objection is that most married opposite-sex couples start off without children, and we do not generally know which couples will have kids and which will not. A temporarily infertile couple may be a prelude to being fertile, and fertile couples always end up infertile. As Maggie Gallagher notes, "Such couples do not contradict in any intelligible, visible way, the basic purposes of marriage as a childrearing institution." Every woman is infertile for most of her life since the fertile window is only a few days per cycle, so fertility cannot be a requirement for marriage.

If fertility is not required for marriage, why should a same-sex couple be banned from marriage on the ground of infertility? This objection confuses what happens usually from what happens always. The *vast majority* of married opposite-sex couples do have biological children together, but no same-sex couple can ever have children together. The law treats what normally happens, not rare exceptions, such as the relatively unusual case of opposite-sex couples without children. The state should not violate the privacy of opposite-sex couples by inquiring about whether they plan to have biological children together, but no same-sex couple can plan to have biological children together. Choices not to procreate children can be changed for opposite-sex couples, but not for same-sex couples. Infertility can be misdiagnosed for opposite-sex couples, but not for same-sex couples.

Judge Walker retorts, "California, like every other state, has never required that individuals entering a marriage be willing or able to procreate." Instead, he writes, "Marriage is the state recognition and approval of a couple's choice to live with each other, to remain committed to one another and to form a household based on their own feelings about one another and to join in an economic partnership and support one another and any dependents." [5]

Walker's statements are in some tension. On the one hand, he denies that marriage is about fertility, because we do not require that married couples try to have babies. If he were consistent, he would also deny that marriage is about committed love, because we do not require that married couples try to remain faithful to one another, insofar as we allow multiple divorce and prenuptial agreements.

In fact, marriage is about committed love and procreation, despite the fact that some married individuals are not willing (or in some cases not able) to remain committed or procreate. For this reason, we rightly reserve marriage to couples who are at least of the proper kind to be able to fulfill these two purposes of marriage.

Similarly, marriage really is about the procreation and education of children, even though not every opposite-sex couple is able to or chooses to have and raise children.

[5] Walker, *Perry v. Schwarzenegger*, p. 67.

A kind of couple intrinsically incapable of committed love (DAM, HAM) cannot marry, nor should the kind of couple that intrinsically excludes children (SEM, SSM).

A final question asked in this debate is, does allowing same-sex marriage harm anyone or anything, including traditional marriage? Advocates for same-sex marriage argue that if some action helps some people and does not harm anyone, it should be allowed. Legalizing same-sex marriage helps the people who want it and does not harm anyone. Therefore, legalizing same-sex marriage should be allowed.

This question can be asked in reply to SSM advocates: How would legalizing self-marriage or polygamy or bigamy harm your unions? As Sherif Girgis, Robert P. George, and Ryan T. Anderson note in the *Harvard Journal of Law & Public Policy*:

> "How would gay marriage affect you or your marriage?" It is worth noting, first, that this question could be turned back on revisionists who oppose legally recognizing, for example, polyamorous unions: How would doing so affect anyone else's marriage? ... [E]ven many revisionists implicitly agree, public institutions like civil marriage have wide and deep effects on our culture—which in turn affects others' lives and choices.[6]

SSM provides a legal approval (not mere toleration) of a kind of sexual activity that is—in the view of many people—inherently immoral. SSM moves society even further from the ideal of marriage as a lifelong union intrinsically ordered to the procreation and education of

---

[6] Girgis, George, and Anderson, "What Is Marriage?", p. 250.

children. If same-sex couples are more likely to be non-monogamous, nonfaithful, and violent,[7] then allowing such couples to marry contributes to undermining the modeling and example that marriage should provide.

Advocates for traditional marriage (TM) hold that legalizing SSM further destabilizes marriage in our society. "People will tend to abide less strictly by any given norms the less those norms make sense. And if marriage is understood as revisionists understand it—that is, as an essentially emotional union that has no principled connection to organic bodily union and the bearing and rearing of children—then marital norms, especially the norms of permanence, monogamy, and fidelity, will make less sense." [8] First, legalizing same-sex marriage may increase rates of divorce among opposite-sex couples, which is to the grave detriment of the children that they have. Even among opposite-sex couples, lack of biological children together is linked to instability in the relationship. Opposite-sex couples procreate 99.999% of children (IVF being the exception); same-sex couples cannot procreate at all (0% of children). David Bess notes:

> Failure to produce children is . . . a leading cause of divorce among humans. Couples with no children divorce far more often than couples with two or more children. According to a United Nations study of millions of people in forty-five societies, 39 percent of divorces occur when there are no children, 26 percent when there is only a single child, 19 percent

[7] See studies cited in Peter Sprigg and Timothy Dailey, *Getting it Straight: What Research Shows About Homosexuality* (Washington DC: Family Research Council, 2004), pp. 103–7.

[8] Girgis, George, and Anderson, "What Is Marriage?", p. 276.

where there are two, and less than 3 percent when there are four or more. The toll on marriage caused by childlessness occurs regardless of the duration of the marriage. Children strengthen marital bonds, reducing the probability of divorce, by creating a powerful commonality of genetic interest between a man and a woman. Failure to produce these small vehicles that transport the genes of both parents into the future deprives a couple of this powerful common bond.[9]

Since same-sex couples cannot have children together, one would expect that their relationships would tend to be less stable. If same-sex couples are granted a legal right to marry, and if they end up divorcing at a rate even higher than opposite-sex couples (which is what one would expect given the importance of shared biological children in keeping a couple together), then divorce would become even more widespread than it currently is. Increases in rates of legal divorce further destabilize marriages that are troubled, since it lends credence to the thought, "Everyone's getting divorced, so we might as well too." The more divorce there is in society, the more socially acceptable it becomes, and the more likely it is that opposite-sex couples will choose divorce over working harder on their marriages.

Secondly, advocates for TM argue that marriage is a prelegal, natural institution that the state merely recognizes (traditional view). Proponents of SSM deny this and hold that marriage is a mere legal construction (nontraditional view) that can and should be changed. Legal approval of SSM endorses the nontraditional view of marriage, thereby

[9] David Bess, *The Evolution of Desire*, 4th ed. (New York: Basic Books, 2003), p. 175.

providing societal disapproval of the traditional view and further socially destabilizing it.

Thirdly, society has an interest in promoting the link between marriage and procreation. It is one thing to say that practices that uncouple marriage and procreation may be permitted by law (not illegal), but it is something much more detrimental to claim that such practices should be encouraged by law. So procreation outside of marriage, such as single parenthood, may be permitted by law (decriminalized), but it should never be promoted by law as is marriage.

Similarly, inherently nonprocreative sexual relationships may be permitted by law, but legalizing SSM promotes a decoupling of marriage and procreation, since same-sex couples cannot engage in actions that are ordered to procreation.

Fourth, society has an interest in promoting the family as a union of a father and a mother, since this form of the family is sociologically proven to be the most beneficial for children.[10] Approval of SSM makes either the father or the mother dispensable in a legally recognized family. Do same-sex couples provide the same benefits to children as opposite-sex couples? We cannot simply assume that because children do better when raised by their married parents they will do equally well being raised by a same-sex couple. There are significant innate, genetic, biological differences between men and women, and therefore between

---

[10] Mark Regnerus, "How Different Are the Adult Children of Parents Who Have Same Sex Relationships? Findings from the New Family Structures Study," *Social Science Research* 41, no. 4 (July 2012), 752–70.

mothers and fathers.[11] Children raised by same-sex couples are always deprived of either their father or their mother.
In a fascinating discussion of why it would be wrong to
conceive a child in order to place the child for adoption,
Bernard G. Prusak argues that parents have imperfect duties
to provide for their own children in ways that only they
can.[12] Prusak provides a framework for coming to the following conclusion: to create children knowing that they
will not have the special care of their mother (or father) is
to fail in an imperfect obligation to the child.[13]

If SSM is legalized, opponents of SSM would be forced
to act against their consciences or be penalized. "In Mas-
sachusetts soon after the state's Supreme Judicial Court in
Goodrich v. Department of Public Health (2003) required that
the state issue marriage licenses to same-sex couples, Catholic Charities, which was at the time in the child adoption
business, was told by the state that it could no longer exclude
same-sex couples as adoptee parents." [14] The children of
advocates of traditional marriage would be taught in public schools about marriage in a way that undermines the
values that are taught in the home. In 2008, a New Jersey
lawsuit forced EHarmony to offer its services to same-sex

[11] See, for example, Steven E. Rhoads, *Taking Sex Differences Seriously* (New
York: Encounter Books, 2005); Leonard Sax, *Why Gender Matters* (New York:
Broadway, 2006); Anne Moir and David Jessel, *Brain Sex: The Real Difference
between Men and Women* (New York: Delta, 1991).

[12] See Bernard G. Prusak, "What Are Parents For?" *Hastings Center Report*
40, no. 2 (2010): 37–47.

[13] The terminology "imperfect" here refers to Immanuel Kant's distinction
of perfect-exceptionless duties and imperfect duties that can admit exceptions.

[14] Francis J. Beckwith, "Same-Sex Marriage and the Failure of Justifica-
tory Liberalism", *First Things*, December 10, 2008, http://www.firstthings.com/
onthesquare/2008/12/same-sex-marriage-and-the-fail.

couples, against the wishes of the company founder, whose research on finding matches had focused only on opposite-sex couples.

SSM advocates believe that SSM is needed to secure important goods for same-sex couples; so even if it is admitted that SSM harms traditional marriage and advocates for traditional marriage, perhaps these harms are justified in light of the greater goods secured through SSM. Numerous empirical studies show that married couples enjoy important goods such as typically living longer, being happier, more stable, and able to visit each other in the hospital. If same-sex couples could marry, they would also live longer, have more stable relationships, and be able to visit each other in the hospital. We have an obligation to help all people secure such important goods. Therefore, we have an obligation to support SSM.

However, SSM may not secure these important goods for same-sex couples. It is true that married couples live longer, are happier, and more stable. But the studies showing these truths of which I am aware are concerning *opposite*-sex couples. As noted earlier, couples of the opposite sex differ in many important ways from couples of the same sex. Marriage benefits for opposite-sex couples may not transfer to same-sex couples. Some benefits certainly would not transfer, such as the benefit for marital stability of having biological children together.

Furthermore, SSM is not needed to secure other important goods for same-sex couples. Marriage is not necessary for visiting someone in the hospital. Outside of medical necessity, the patient decides who can visit in the hospital. If the patient is unconscious, legal documents can secure the right of proxy health-care decision making and right of access for *whomever* the patient wishes. Similarly, legal documents can secure other material goods that a couple (same sex or opposite sex) might want to share.

To sum up, three major questions arose in considering the issues of same-sex marriage. Is a ban on same-sex marriage like a ban on interracial marriage? In fact, banning SSM is not like banning interracial marriage, for we commonly accept treating differences in sex in ways that we do not accept for race. Secondly, the premises that justify SSM also "prove" the legitimacy of bigamy, polygamy, polyamory, and self-marriage, with some but not all arguments also applying to marriage between humans and nonhumans. And finally, if SSM were legalized, it would really harm advocates for traditional marriage as well as the institution of marriage itself.

The Seventh Big Myth

Priestly Celibacy Caused the Crisis of Sexual Abuse of Minors: The Myth of Priestly Pedophilia

At least three significant questions arise in connection with the subject of priestly celibacy and sexual abuse of minors. First, does priestly celibacy cause the sexual abuse of children? Second, why are priests forced to be celibate? And third, what caused the sex abuse crisis in the Church? This chapter will attempt to provide answers to these important questions.

First, and Perhaps Most Importantly, Does Celibacy for Priests Cause the Sexual Abuse of Children?

Judge Richard Posner writes, "The problem of priests' sexually molesting boys would be solved if priests were allowed to marry."[1] Is it true that if Catholic priests were allowed to marry, then the sexual abuse of children by priests would not have taken place?

---

[1] Richard Posner, "Contraception and Catholicism", November 28, 2010, http://www.becker-posner-blog.com/2010/11/contraception-and-catholicismposner.html (accessed December 15, 2010).

Many people have investigated this question, and the answer is clear. In *Psychology Today*, Michael Castleman's article "Beyond Bad-Apple Priests: Who the Pedophiles Really Are" pointed out, "From media reports, one might infer that Catholic priests commit most pedophilia. In fact, only a tiny fraction of child sex abusers are priests." [2] Dr. Philip Jenkins, Distinguished Professor of History and Religious Studies at Penn State, author of *Pedophiles and Priests: Anatomy of a Contemporary Crisis* published by Oxford University Press, states:

> My research of cases over the past 20 years indicates no evidence whatever that Catholic or other celibate clergy are any more likely to be involved in misconduct or abuse than clergy of any other denomination—or indeed, than nonclergy. However determined news media may be to see this affair as a crisis of celibacy, the charge is just unsupported.... My concern over the "pedophile priest" issue is not to defend evil clergy, or a sinful church (I cannot be called a Catholic apologist, since I am not even a Catholic). But I am worried that justified anger over a few awful cases might be turned into ill-focused attacks against innocent clergy. The story of clerical misconduct is bad enough without turning into an unjustifiable outbreak of religious bigotry against the Catholic Church. [3]

Ernie Allen, president of the National Center for Missing and Exploited Children, notes: "We don't see the

[2] Michael Castleman, "Beyond Bad-Apple Priests: Who the Pedophiles Really Are", http://www.psychologytoday.com/blog/all-about-sex/201003/beyond-bad-apple-priests-who-the-pedophiles-really-are (accessed July 25, 2011).

[3] Philip Jenkins, "Myth of the Pedophile Priest", *Zenit*, March 11, 2002, http://www.zenit.org/article-3922?l=english (accessed July 25, 2011).

Catholic Church as a hotbed of this [abuse] or a place that has a bigger problem than anyone else. I can tell you without hesitation that we have seen cases in many religious settings, from traveling evangelists to mainstream ministers to rabbis and others." [4] Also supportive of this conclusion is Professor of Psychology Dr. Thomas Plante, who writes in *Psychology Today*:

> Catholic clergy aren't more likely to abuse children than other clergy or men in general. According to the best available data (which is pretty good mostly coming from a comprehensive report by the John Jay College of Criminal Justice in 2004 as well as several other studies), 4% of Catholic priests in the USA sexually victimized minors during the past half century. No evidence has been published at this time that states that this number is higher than clergy from other religious traditions. The 4% figure is lower than school teachers (at 5%) during the same time frame and perhaps as much as half of the numbers of the general population of men. [5]

Insurance companies stay in business by calculating the likelihood of various events taking place, including death, car accidents, and abuse. They have a huge financial interest in objective standards of evidence. In 2010, *Newsweek* reported:

---

[4] Quoted in "Mean Men" by Pat Wingert, *Newsweek*, April 7, 2010, http://www.thedailybeast.com/newsweek/2010/04/07/mean-men.html (accessed January 12, 2012).

[5] Thomas G. Plante, Ph.D., "Six Important Points You Don't Hear about regarding Clergy Sexual Abuse in the Catholic Church", *Psychology Today*, March 24, 2010, http://www.psychologytoday.com/blog/do-the-right-thing/201003/six-important-points-you-dont-hear-about-regarding-clergy-sexual-abus (accessed July 25, 2011).

> Since the mid-1980s, insurance companies have offered sexual misconduct coverage as a rider on liability insurance, and their own studies indicate that Catholic churches are not higher risk than other congregations. Insurance companies that cover all denominations, such as Guide One Center for Risk Management, which has more than 40,000 church clients, does not charge Catholic churches higher premiums.[6]

The evidence is substantial and confirmed by psychologists, researchers, and insurance companies: priestly celibacy is not a risk factor for the sexual abuse of children.

Although media reports focus on sexual abuse by Catholic clergy to a greater extent than they focus on other perpetrators of sexual abuse, in fact a much greater percentage of sexual abuse takes place within families than by clergy of any denomination. A cohabiting boyfriend or stepfather is a much more likely perpetrator of abuse than a Catholic priest. In the mass media, there are frequent calls to discontinue celibacy for clergy, but no commentators have called for the abolition of cohabitation or an end to divorce and remarriage.

Unfortunately, sexual abuse of minors is also common in schools. Dr. Charol Shakeshaft, a researcher at Hofstra University, examined abuse rates in schools and found serious problems. "[T]hink the Catholic Church has a problem?" she said. "The physical sexual abuse of students in schools is likely more than 100 times the abuse by priests."[7] Here again, the inconsistent treatment of

---

[6] Wingert, "Mean Men".

[7] Quoted in "Sex Abuse by Teachers Said Worse than Catholic Church", by Jon E. Dougherty, *NewsMax.com*, April 5, 2004, http://archive.newsmax.com/archives/articles/2004/4/5/01552.shtml (accessed July 25, 2011).

this issue by the press is evident, for headlines do not warn people about the grave danger of "pedophile teachers". Tom Hoopes notes: "The 2002 Department of Education report estimated that from 6 percent to 10 percent of all students in public schools would be victims of abuse before graduation—a staggering statistic."[8] He continues, "Yet, during the first half of 2002, the 61 largest newspapers in California ran nearly 2,000 stories about sexual abuse in Catholic institutions, mostly concerning past allegations. During the same period, those newspapers ran four stories about the federal government's discovery of the much larger—and ongoing—abuse scandal in public schools."[9]

None of these facts are meant to excuse or belittle the reality and problem of sexual abuse by Catholic clergy. Sexual abuse of a minor by anyone is intrinsically evil according to the moral law and a serious crime according to the civil law. No situation, no motive, or no excuse can justify it—ethically or legally—under any circumstances. The identity of the priestly abuser compounds the evil done. Like a church building or a chalice, priests are consecrated to the service of God, and like a church building or chalice, it is possible to make sacrilegious use of what is consecrated to the service of God. Theologian Germain Grisez notes that because the body of the priest is consecrated to the service of God, "all violations of the sixth commandment by or with anyone who

---

[8] Tom Hoopes, "Has Media Ignored Sex Abuse in School?", *CBS News*, August 24, 2006, http://www.cbsnews.com/stories/2006/08/24/opinion/main1933687.shtml (accessed July 25, 2011).

[9] Ibid.

has undertaken celibate chastity for the kingdom's sake are also sacrileges." [10]

Clerical abuse adds to this immorality a further deformity of the betrayal of trust in virtue of the position of care and responsibility that priests have for the people to whom they offer spiritual care. "It is a betrayal of trust comparable to treason against one's country", writes Grisez; "It always risks seriously injuring the spiritual goods for which the Church is responsible—goods immeasurably more precious than human life itself. The injury done to the victim's spiritual wellbeing is likely to be serious and might well be pastorally irremediable." [11] When discovered by others, clerical abuse also undermines the public perception of priests, the openness of people to hearing the Gospel, and the readiness of some of the faithful to come to the sacraments, especially confession. The abuse of minors by anyone is always unethical and always illegal, but the abuse of minors by priests compounds the wrongdoing.

It is also always wrong to falsely accuse or defame the innocent. The vast majority of priests—like the vast majority of teachers and parents—work for the well-being of others and have never engaged in abuse of any kind. It is unfair to single out and stereotype Catholic clergy as if they were as a group depraved and perverted. Every large group of people—doctors, teachers, gardeners, coaches, or priests—will have some percentage of "bad apples".

---

[10] Germain Grisez, "*Sin, Grace, and Zero Tolerance: An Exchange*", with a reply by Avery Cardinal Dulles, S.J., *First Things* 151 (Mar 2005): 27–36, at 29.

[11] Ibid., p. 30.

Priests—like all people—should not be punished or assumed guilty until proven innocent. Although a small minority of priests have perpetrated sexual abuse, the vast majority of priests are innocent of these crimes. Like the vast majority of teachers, doctors, and coaches, they are innocent and should be treated in accordance with who they are—honorable people who are trying to provide a valuable service to the human community.

Still, celibacy itself is an issue for many people. Although it is clear that abolishing celibacy for priests would not eliminate sexual abuse, since married clergy in other denominations have also been found guilty of sexual abuse, many people have important concerns about celibacy itself.

Why Are Catholic Priests Forced to Be Celibate?

This question involves a misunderstanding. No one is "forced" to be celibate, since no one is forced to be a Catholic priest. Priests freely choose to embrace the commitment of celibacy for the sake of serving God's Kingdom in a heroic way. Such a decision is similar to joining the Marine Corps. In joining the priesthood or the Marines, a person volunteers for an arduous undertaking for the sake of serving God or country in an extraordinary way.

History provides other examples of people foregoing the goods of marriage and sex in order single-mindedly to pursue a mission of great purpose. Dag Hammarskjöld, the first Secretary General of the United Nations, embraced celibacy in order more fruitfully and intensely to seek world peace. Mahatma Gandhi chose celibacy as part of his quest for freedom for his country. George Frideric Handel never married so as to focus on his musical composition. Catholic priests choose celibacy as a way of loving God and neighbor, as a way of imitating Jesus, as a way of bearing witness.

Before becoming Pope Benedict XVI, Joseph Cardinal Ratzinger had this to say about the meaning of religious celibacy:

> The renunciation of marriage and family is thus to be understood in terms of this vision: I renounce what, humanly speaking, is not only the most normal but also the most important thing. I forego bringing forth further life on the tree of life, and I live in the faith that my land is really God—and so I make it easier for others, also, to believe that there is a kingdom of heaven. I bear witness to Jesus Christ, to the Gospel, not only with words, but also with a specific mode of existence, and I place my life in this form at his disposal. . . . The point is really an existence that stakes everything on God and leaves out precisely the one thing that normally makes a human existence fulfilled with a promising future.[12]

The priest gives witness, not merely by words, but even by his own way of living, to the priority above all things of serving God.

The witness of evangelical celibacy is powerful. As mentioned earlier, Blessed John Henry Cardinal Newman once spoke of "the Ventures of Faith". What if it turned out that the Christian creed was mistaken? What if Jesus were not

---

[12] Joseph Ratzinger, *Salt of the Earth: Christianity and the Catholic Church at the End of the Millennium; An Interview with Peter Seewald* (San Francisco: Ignatius Press, 1997), p. 195.

God; what if there were no God? Would it make any difference to your life? If the answer is no, if nothing in your life would be changed if the Gospel were mere fables, then you have not yet made a venture in faith. Celibacy for the sake of the Kingdom of God (not merely abstaining from sex for other reasons) makes sense only on the supposition that a person embraces a great venture of faith. One person acting in such a way can have a profound effect on the life of faith of other people. We are inspired in life by the heroic actions of others, and the greater the sacrificial deeds, the greater the potential to move others. The celibate priest may have no biological children of his own, but he ought to be greatly fruitful in spiritual children, who are moved by his deeds of kindness and, yes, by his great sacrificial love, which inspires them to deeper love as well.

The freely made decision of celibacy scandalizes some people. Father Richard John Neuhaus noted, "The celibacy rule is so offensive to many of today's commentators, Catholic and otherwise, because it so frontally challenges the culturally entrenched dogma that human fulfillment and authenticity are impossible without sexual intercourse of one kind or another." [13] In a culture that often preaches through television, movies, and songs that sexual fulfillment is a necessary good, the religious celibate will seem to be a heretic. In a culture such as ours, the heroic witness of persons foregoing marriage and sex in order to bear testimony in deeds to the primacy of the Gospel is more important than ever.

---

[13] Quoted by Mary Eberstadt, "The Elephant in the Sacristy", *The Weekly Standard* 7, no. 39 (June 17, 2002), http://www.weeklystandard.com/Content/Public/Articles/000/000/001/344fsdzu.asp?page=3.

But can't a person serve God, heroically serve God, without being celibate? Of course. Indeed, heroically to love God and neighbor is the call, not just of priests or nuns, but of every baptized person. Still, there are important differences in the mode of life of a person celibately consecrated to God and a married person. Let's compare, for example, a married man and a celibate priest.

A married man and a celibate priest should both love God above all things, but their way of expressing this love is importantly different. A married man should express his love for God by giving a special priority—above all other people—to his wife. In second place, after his wife, he should love his own children. The properly ordered love of a married man puts the welfare of his family in pride of place. His way of loving God is expressed through his preferential and sacrificial love for his wife, and after her, his children. A husband who neglected properly loving his wife and children, who sought to do "great things" for others in his work or in his parish, but failed in his first responsibility, would be acting badly. A man's own children and wife have a special claim on his attention, his energy, and his service, a claim that other people cannot make. A father and husband has a special responsibility to look after the well-being of his wife and children and to put their needs ahead of his wants and the desires of the larger community.

In not having a spouse and children, the sacrificial love of the celibate priest is diffused, less particular, and more universal. For Catholics, each priest is a "Father", and the Church community is his bride. Laypeople have special claims on priestly fathers to look after their spiritual well-being, to hear their confessions, to help them on their journey to God. It is fitting that the priest be without his own biological children—as a father available and responsible for a great many spiritual children. In a sense, everyone is his son or daughter, his priority, the one to whom he should especially devote his care. The Church is his bride, and he will often be called to make great sacrifices in terms of his time, energy, and service for her well-being. The celibate priest can serve whoever has the greatest need, wherever he can make the greatest contribution, and however it best serves the common good.

By contrast, a husband and a father must first serve his own family and would act badly if he alleviated the greatest need by putting his own children in need. A married man cannot give away all his money to the poor without making his own family destitute. A priest can. The married man cannot move to Africa to serve orphans whose parents have died of AIDS without putting his family in jeopardy. A priest can. A husband and father makes his primary contribution to the well-being of the world via his family, by serving his wife and his children. A husband and father serves the common good by means of first taking care of the private good of those for whom he is primarily responsible. A celibate priest can make whoever it is that has the greatest physical or spiritual need his "family". He serves the common good directly. Like marriage, the acceptance of priestly celibacy is a free choice—undertaken for the sake of Love—but unlike the married man, the love (*agape*) of a priest is not particular and individualized to focus particularly on one woman, on one family, but universal and widely diffused.

What Caused the Sex Abuse Crisis in the Church?

The late Richard John Neuhaus wrote: "This crisis is about three things: fidelity, fidelity, fidelity." [14] If priests had kept their vows to God, if they had been faithful to their own commitments to those they served, if they had simply obeyed canon law and civil law, there would have been no sexual abuse. It was not *celibacy* that caused the problem, but rather a *lack of celibacy*. The gross sin and criminal misconduct of a small minority of priests damaged the lives of the young people abused, undermined the spiritual well-being of the community, and cost millions of dollars—much of which has gone to trial lawyers, rather than victims. The primary cause of the problem rests with a small minority of clergy who radically contradicted the priestly vocation of loving, sacrificial service.

Unfortunately, a lack of fidelity was also evident among many bishops. As Pope Benedict XVI pointed out to the bishops of Ireland,[15] many bishops failed to enforce canon law, which requires that serious crimes such as child abuse be met with serious punishments. Instead, many bishops treated sexual abuse in ways that were merely therapeutic. Many bishops did not take allegations of abuse seriously, and many bishops did not punish those who abused (as canon law required) but simply moved them to new

[14] Richard John Neuhaus, "Scandal Time (Continued)", *First Things*, June/July 2002, http://www.firstthings.com/ftissues/ft0206/public.html.
[15] Pope Benedict XVI, "Pastoral Letter of the Holy Father Pope Benedict XVI to the Catholics of Ireland", March 19, 2010, vatican.va/holy_father/Benedict?XVI/letters/2010/documents/hf_ben_xvi_let_20100319_ireland_en.html.

opportunities to abuse. Beginning in the 1960s, there was a laxity in discipline in the Church and a negligence in enforcing the behavior appropriate for clergy. The National Review Board, appointed to investigate the crisis, noted "moral laxity, excessive leniency" as part of the cause of the crisis.[16]

Happily, this situation has now been rectified, at least with respect to sexual abuse of minors. The norms accepted by the U.S. Bishops in 2002 require *zero tolerance* of sexual abuse: "When even a single act of sexual abuse by a priest or deacon is admitted or is established after an appropriate process in accord with canon law, the offending priest or deacon will be removed permanently from ecclesiastical ministry."[17] The Catholic Church in the United States has taken extensive measures to prevent child abuse, measures that are highly effective. George Weigel writes, "Catholicism has cleaned house in America, where the church is likely the country's safest environment for young people today (there were six credible cases of abuse reported in 2009: six too many, but remarkably low in a community of some 68 million members)."[18] By way of comparison, the *New York Post* reported, "At least one child is sexually abused by a school

[16] Robert S. Bennett, et al., *A Report on the Crisis in the Catholic Church in the United States*, prepared by the National Review Board for the Protection of Children and Young People (Washington, D.C.: USCCB, 2004), p. 92.

[17] United States Conference of Catholic Bishops, "Essential Norms for Diocesan/Eparchial Policies Dealing with Allegations of Sexual Abuse of Minors by Priests or Deacons", June 16, 2011, http://old.usccb.org/ocyp/charter.pdf, no. 8.

[18] George Weigel, "Church Gets an Unfair Rap", *Philadelphia Inquirer*, April 11, 2010, http://m.sunjournal.com/node/827390.

employee every day in New York City schools." [19] The situation of the Catholic Church with respect to the crime of child abuse is much better than other institutions. Virtually all the cases of abuse connected to the Church now talked about in the mass media involve cases that are thirty, forty, or even fifty years old.

Another part of the laxity of many bishops with respect to sexual abuse involved a failure to teach properly. There was ambiguity with respect to celibacy as taught in seminaries and also in "updating" classes following Vatican II. Notre Dame Professor Ralph McInerny, in his autobiography *I Alone Have Escaped to Tell You*, recounts a telling experience after Vatican II:

> A St. Paul priest I had known years before, who had been engaged in dedicated and effective pastoral work, came to Notre Dame to be renewed. We had lunch one day in the University Club. After pleasant reminiscing, it became clear he wanted to talk about what he was undergoing. He leaned across the table and said to me in a whisper, "They told us to forget everything we had been taught in the seminary." Perhaps the one speaking to those priests was indulging in hyperbole, a little rhetorical excess to gain attention. Perhaps. The effect on my old friend was obvious.... Now he was being told to forget everything that had defined his life. How could he not feel vertigo? He finished the course and went home and a few years later left the priesthood, under a cloud of accusations of sexual irregularity. [20]

[19] Douglas Montero, "Secret Shame of Our Schools: Sexual Abuse of Students Runs Rampant", *The New York Post*, July 30, 2001, http://www.nypost.com/p/news/item_IGmFG437dEYB9jg6CAY6TO.

[20] Ralph McInerny, *I Alone Have Escaped to Tell You: My Life and Pastimes* (Notre Dame: University of Notre Dame Press, 2006), p. 130. For more on Ralph McInerny, see Christopher Kaczor's *O Rare Ralph McInerny: Stories*

Both within the Church and in culture generally, an excessive laxity with respect to sexual ethics helps explain why rates of abuse exploded at a particular time—the late sixties and seventies—and then began to fall dramatically in the eighties to much lower levels. The following chart from the National Review Board indicates the counts of sexual abuse and the number of priests involved according to year.[21]

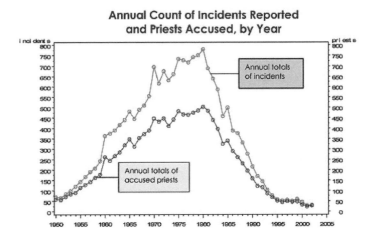

Annual Count of Incidents Reported and Priests Accused, by Year

Cases of abuse were relatively rare in the 1950s and became rare again in the late 1980s and 1990s. There was an explosive increase in abuse during the 1960s and 1970s, a time

---

and Reflections on a Legendary Notre Dame Professor (South Bend, Ind.: St. Augustine's Press, 2011).

[21] From http://douthat.blogs.nytimes.com/2010/03/30/the-pattern-of-priestly-sex-abuse/ (downloaded on July 25, 2011).

of widespread rejection of traditional teaching about sexual ethics in society generally and in the Church in particular. Rather than ensure, as was their duty, that the Church's doctrines and disciplines were clearly taught and firmly enforced, many bishops turned a blind eye. Mostly by their inaction, many bishops allowed an "openness" to the reigning libertine spirit to be fostered unchecked among seminarians and clergy.

The primary blame for the crisis rests on those priests who lacked fidelity to their vows; secondary blame rests with those bishops who lacked fidelity in governing the Church in accordance with canon and civil law, in teaching sound doctrine, and in making sure that others in their dioceses taught sound doctrine; and thirdly—a distant third in my view—some laypeople contributed to the problem of sexual abuse by clericalism. Russell Shaw defines *clericalism* as

> an elitist mindset, together with structures and patterns of behavior corresponding to it, which takes it for granted that clerics—in the Catholic context, mainly bishops and priests—are intrinsically superior to the other members of the Church and deserve automatic deference. Passivity and dependence are the laity's lot. By no means is clericalism confined to clerics themselves. The clericalist mindset is widely shared by Catholic lay people.[22]

In some cases, clericalism led some clerics and some lay people to deny there was a problem at all, or to deny that the problem was as grave as it was, or not to

[22] Quoted in "The Scandal of Clericalism" by Carl Olson, *Ignatius Insight Scoop*, February 2008, http://insightscoop.typepad.com/2004/2008/02/the-scandal-of.html.

take appropriate action in response to allegations. In some cases, for example, police officers did not enforce the law and prosecutors did not file charges on account of an improper deference to clergy. (It is inconsistent that critics of the Church do not also call to task police departments and district attorneys who behaved in this way. Often the police acted as did many bishops—but no one seems to be similarly outraged, despite the fact that police officers, and not bishops, take an oath to enforce the law.) As Father Neuhaus notes, "Faithful Catholics owe it to the Church and owe it to their bishops not to let them off the hook. In this instance, the virtue of docility includes a respect for bishops that requires recalling them to the duty and the dignity to which they were ordained. Too many of them have neglected that duty and debased that dignity."[23] In a fitting way, laypeople have not only the right but the duty to correct and to call to fidelity ordained clergy and bishops who neglect or even contradict their vocation to serve.

In summing up the issue, Richard Neuhaus said it best:

At the epicenter of the continuing crisis is the simple, however difficult, virtue of fidelity. What is this crisis about? The answer is that this crisis is about three things: fidelity, fidelity, and fidelity. The fidelity of bishops and priests to the teaching of the Church and to their solemn vows; the fidelity of bishops in exercising oversight in ensuring obedience to that teaching and to those vows; and the fidelity of the lay faithful in holding bishops and priests accountable.[24]

[23] Neuhaus, "Scandal Time (Continued)".
[24] Ibid.

The real issue was never celibacy, but rather fidelity, or rather, the unfortunate lack of fidelity. The sexual abuse of minors represents one of the most horrible and blatant of sins. The scandal was caused by a lack of living in accordance with what the Church teaches. Indeed, if priests and lay people accepted and faithfully lived what the Church teaches about happiness, love, and sexuality, sexual abuse of minors would be entirely nonexistent.